I'm a Vegetarian

Amazing facts and ideas for healthy vegetarians

Ellen Schwartz, 1949-
Illustrated by Farida Zaman

Tundra Books

Published in Canada by Tundra Books,
481 University Avenue, Toronto, Ontario M5G 2E9

Published in the United States by Tundra Books of Northern New York,
P.O. Box 1030, Plattsburgh, New York 12901

Library of Congress Control Number: 2001095376

National Library of Canada Cataloguing in Publication Data

Schwartz, Ellen, 1949-
  I'm a vegetarian : amazing facts and ideas for healthy vegetarians

ISBN 0-88776-588-2

1. Vegetarianism – Juvenile literature. I. Zaman, Farida II. Title.

TX392.S38 2002   613.2'62   C2001-903420-2

We acknowledge the support of the Canada Council for the Arts and
the Ontario Arts Council for our publishing program.

We acknowledge the financial support of the Government of Canada
through the Book Publishing Industry Development Program for our
publishing activities.

Design: Blaine Herrmann

Printed and bound in Canada

1 2 3 4 5 6   07 06 05 04 03 02

Acknowledgments

The author would like to thank the following people:

For reviewing portions of the manuscript and providing feedback:
Elissa Greenfield, Jenna Greenfield, Laura Greenfield, Susan Hutcheon,
Reed Mangels and the Vegetarian Resource Group, Hannah Milstein,
Rachel Rosenberg, Merri Schwartz, Diane Stebner, Grant Stebner, and
especially, for her invaluable help, Brenda Davis.

For providing recipes: Amy Schwartz.

For research assistance: Bill Schwartz.

For the generous use of a place to write: James and Lynn Hill.

For interviews and quotations: Carolynne Burkholder, Brianna Craven,
Jesse Megan Gray, Leanne Humphrey, Liv Lundh, and Jesse Ross.

For permission to use quotations: the American Dietetic Association;
James Cromwell; Janet Rasmussen, Windstar Communications (for John
Denver); Alan Durning and the Worldwatch Institute (www.worldwatch.org);
Richard Melville Hall (commonly known as Moby); Paul Hawken; and
Frances Moore Lappé.

The author is indebted to the following sources of information:

Becoming Vegetarian by Vesanto Melina, Brenda Davis and Victoria Harrison.

Food: Feasts, Cooks and Kitchens by Richard Tames.

"How Many Teens Are Vegetarian? How Many Kids Don't Eat Meat?"
Vegetarian Journal, Volume XIX, Number 6, January/February 2001, page 10.

"The Origins of Modern Vegetarianism" from *The New Vegetarians* by Paul R.
Amato, and Sonia A. Partridge. From www.eatveg.com.

"Our Food, Our Planet" by EarthSave. From www.earthsave.bc.ca.

Spill the Beans and Pass the Peanuts: Legumes by Meredith Sayles Hughes.

A Teen's Guide to Going Vegetarian by Judy Krizmanic.

Tomatoes, Potatoes, Corn and Beans by Sylvia A. Johnson.

"Vegan Nutrition in Pregnancy and Childhood" by Reed Mangels and Katie
Kavanagh-Prochaska and the Vegetarian Resource Group at www.vrg.org.

"Vegetarian Nutrition for Teenagers" from the Vegetarian Resource Group
at www.vrg.org.

"Vegetarian Facts and Fiction" by Carol Wiley. In *Vegetarian Times*.

For Merri and Amy
E.S.

For Layla and Gibran, with love.
Happy, healthy eating!
F.Z.

Contents

So You've Decided to Be a Vegetarian

What do Julia Stiles, Leonardo da Vinci, and Moby have in common? How about Albert Einstein, Drew Barrymore, and David Bowie?

If you guessed they're all vegetarians, you're right. And so are thousands of other celebrities – actors and musicians, scientists and artists, athletes and inventors. And so are millions of ordinary people across North America and around the world.

In fact, vegetarianism is a growing worldwide trend. Just consider these facts:

♦ Approximately 13 million North Americans are vegetarians, and a million more join their ranks every year.

♦ Experts say kids in their teens are the fastest-growing group of vegetarians.

♦ More than one million North American kids in the 6 to 17 age bracket have said "no" to meat.

♦ Vegetarianism has gone mainstream. Compared to just a few years ago, there are more vegetarian restaurants, more meatless dishes on restaurant menus, and more vegetarian foods in grocery stores than ever before.

In the past, some people considered vegetarians to be weird cultists who ate nothing but seaweed and granola. Today, a diet that focuses on grains, legumes, fruits, and vegetables is not just seen as normal, it's considered desirable and healthy.

And it *is* healthy. In fact, the American Dietetic Association stated in 1997, "It *is* the position of the American Dietetic Association that appropriately planned vegetarian diets are healthful, are nutritionally adequate, and provide health benefits in the pre-vention and treatment of certain diseases."

Of course, eating isn't just about health. It's also about good taste and energy and fun. A vegetarian diet can supply all of those things, too. And talk about adventure – adopting a meat-free diet can be the beginning of a delicious food tour around the globe.

Whether you are a lifelong vegetarian or vegan, or a brand-new one, this book is for you. In these pages, you'll meet kids like 11-year-old Brianna, 13-year-old Tim, and 15-year-old Jesse. You'll find out why they went vegetarian and what they like about it. You'll discover how to win over your parents, how to make your school more veggie-friendly, and how to handle sticky situations – such as Thanksgiving dinner, when Aunt Erma is begging you to "try a turkey leg, for my sake" and Uncle Fred is warning of your imminent demise if you don't "smarten up and eat your meat!" You'll learn nutrition basics to help you plan a vegetarian diet that's healthy for growing bodies. And you'll find delicious recipes to get you started in the world of meatless cooking.

So, welcome to a different way of eating – and of living. A way that's compassionate to animals, kind to the environment, healthy and tasty and fun. In the words of the Irish playwright George Bernard Shaw, a lifelong vegetarian who lived to be 94: "Animals are my friends – and I don't eat my friends."

I'm a Vegetarian and I Feel Great!

What is a Vegetarian, Anyway?

Before we talk about how to be a vegetarian, we've got to know what a vegetarian is. So here's a basic definition:

A vegetarian is a person who eats no meat of any kind – no beef, pork, lamb, poultry, or fish. A vegetarian diet may include animal products such as eggs, dairy products (such as milk, cheese, and yogurt), and honey.

Simple, right? Not so fast. Within the basic definition, there are several sub-categories.

Lacto-ovo vegetarian: *Lacto* means milk and *ovo* means egg, so – you guessed it – a lacto-ovo vegetarian eats dairy products and eggs, but no meat. About 95 percent of all vegetarians in North America are this type. So, for the obvious sub-sub-categories...

Lacto vegetarian: A vegetarian who eats dairy products but no eggs.

Ovo vegetarian: A vegetarian who eats eggs but no dairy products.

Vegan: A vegan is a person who does not use any animal products for food or clothing. That means not only do vegans eat no meat, milk, or eggs, but also they consume and use no honey, leather, wool, silk, or down. Veganism is not just a diet, it's a way of life that avoids exploiting animals in any way.

Macrobiotic: A macrobiotic diet follows a Japanese philosophy based on principles of eating, such as balancing the energy in foods, rather than on including or excluding certain foods. Most macrobiotic diets are vegetarian, although some include fish.

Fruitarian: Just the way it sounds, a fruitarian diet consists of only fruits, including tomatoes, squash, seeds, and nuts. Even with these foods, a fruitarian diet is not considered healthy.

Semi-vegetarian: Some people mainly follow a vegetarian diet but eat small amounts of meat, poultry, or fish. They might call themselves vegetarians, although they are not true vegetarians. *Pesco* means fish, and *pollo* means chicken, so pesco vegetarians and pollo vegetarians are – well, you can figure it out.

Why Do Kids Go Vegetarian?

You name it – that's why kids go vegetarian.

Some kids are lifelong vegetarians. Their parents are vegetarians and they were raised that way. Even when the kids get old enough to make their own choices, they stick with it because they like the meat-free way of eating.

Other kids become vegetarians on their own. Something triggers the idea for them and they decide to make a change.

10

Either way, it's a personal decision. There's no right or wrong reason, no right or wrong way to go about it. You have to decide what feels right and what works for you.

Here are the main reasons that kids give.

Animal Rights

I have, from an early age, renounced eating meat: the time will come when men such as I will look upon the murder of animals as they now look upon the murder of men.

Leonardo da Vinci, artist

Animals are dumb unfeeling creatures put on earth to serve and feed people, right? *Wrong!* say millions of kids. In fact, the biggest reason many young people become vegetarians is out of concern for animal rights. They believe that animals have just as much right to live as people, and that humans don't have the right to exploit or kill animals just to satisfy their own desires. And they don't object only to killing animals for food, but also to the way animals are treated in the food industry.

Brianna, 11: *When I was younger, I used to look at the food on my plate and ask, "Mommy, what am I eating?" but my parents didn't want to tell me. But when I was six, I figured it out for myself and said, "I'm not eating this anymore." I feel so much better not eating animals. Now I can feel good about what I eat.*

Jesse, 15: *Personally, I think it's cruel to kill and eat cows and chickens when there is other food available. I can understand if it's a matter of life or death, and you need to kill something to avoid starving. But when cows are being slaughtered by the hundreds every day in a factory so you can enjoy a Big Mac, I think that's just plain wrong.*

11

Megan, 22: I went to a friend's house for dinner and I watched her mom dismember a chicken. That was when it hit home that it was a real animal. On the spot I decided not to eat meat anymore. In fact, I refused to eat the dinner, and my friend's mom was so angry she sent me home!

Did You Know?

- Every year, in the U.S. and Canada, seven billion animals – not including fish – are slaughtered for food. That's more creatures than there are people on earth!
- Every average North American man, woman, and child consumes 35 animals a year. Over a lifetime, that adds up to 2555 chickens and turkeys, 33 pigs, and 12 cattle and calves.
- Most food animals are raised in cages and pens that are too small for them. Often, they have no room to walk or even turn around.

Try This

Grab a ruler and a sheet of paper. Trace a square 6 inches (15 cm) on each side. That's how much space the average chicken gets in a typical egg-laying factory cage.

If any kid ever realized what was involved in factory farming, they would never touch meat again. I was so moved by the intelligence, sense of fun and personalities of the animals I worked with on Babe *that by the end of the film I was a vegan.*

James Cromwell, actor

The Environment

Livestock production is the most ecologically damaging component of American agriculture.

Alan Durning,
senior researcher at the Worldwatch Institute

At first glance, there doesn't seem to be much connection between meat and the environment. Farmers raise livestock, the animals are slaughtered, the meat is shipped to market, and people buy it and eat it. But have you ever thought about what happens to the environment as a result of this seemingly simple process? The production of meat uses vast amounts of land, water, and energy. It contributes to soil erosion, the spread of deserts, and the destruction of rain forests. It causes water and air pollution. No wonder so many "green" kids are making the switch to a meatless diet.

Tim, 13: *I was watching this show about the Amazon. It said that in South America, an area of rain forest the size of the country of Wales was destroyed every year for cattle ranching — mostly for fast-food restaurants in North America. That really shook me up. All of a sudden I realized that what I ate had an impact on the environment — on the wilderness I loved! So I decided to stop eating meat. I'm not saving the rain forest, but at least my diet is helping.*

Did You Know?

◆ It takes 10 times more water, and 10 to 20 times more energy, to produce beef as it does to produce the same amount of wheat. It takes less water and energy to produce food for a vegetarian for a year than to produce food for a meat-eater for a month.

- We know that cars and factories produce greenhouse gases – but did you know that livestock does, too? Animal manure releases greenhouse gases, which contribute to global warming.

- The United Nations reports that all 17 of the world's major fishing areas have been harvested at or beyond their natural limits. And it's not just fish that are affected. Often, fishing nets catch – and kill – whales, seals, and dolphins.

Try This

Go to an atlas and locate the American state of New Jersey. That's the size of a "dead zone" in the Gulf of Mexico. The cause of this lifeless area? Runoff containing fertilizers and pesticides flows from farms down the Mississippi River into the Gulf, where it kills or chokes out plants and animals.

Basically we should stop doing those things that are destructive to the environment, other creatures, and ourselves, and figure out new ways of existing.

Moby, musician

Besides being easy, delicious, economical, and healthful, a plant-based diet transforms your fork into a powerful tool for environmental protection and restoration.

Paul Hawken, author

Health

He is a heavy eater of meat. Me thinks it doth harm to his wit.

William Shakespeare,
playwright, in *Twelfth Night*

"Don't stop eating meat! You'll get sick! You'll starve! You'll get weak! You'll shrivel up and die!" Not long ago, that was the general view of vegetarianism. Now we know that the opposite is true – a vegetarian diet, as long as it's nutritionally balanced, is actually better for you than a diet that contains meat. And the fear that children raised on a vegetarian diet will be sickly and scrawny is disproved by evidence that vegetarian kids grow and thrive at a healthy rate. Liv is a good example. Now 17, she's a lifelong vegetarian, along with the rest of her family. Why does she stay meat-free? "I feel healthier," she says.

Did You Know?

- Vegetarians are less likely than meat-eaters to get heart disease, certain types of cancer, diabetes, osteoporosis (brittle bones), and other diseases.
- Vegetarians often report that they have more energy and alertness than meat-eaters, and they're generally less obese.
- Eighty per cent of North American meat contains drugs – antibiotics fed to animals to prevent diseases that spread in crowded conditions, hormones given to make animals grow faster, and chemicals from pesticides sprayed on the grain that animals eat. Scientists don't know whether these substances are safe for humans.

What did the tired tomato say to the lazy lettuce?

Let's veg out.

15

◆ Vegetarians avoid harmful bacteria and viruses found in meat. These include disease-causing salmonella bacteria, found in improperly cooked meat and fish, and viruses such as the one that causes "mad cow disease."

It's nice to eat a meal and not have to worry about what your food may have died of.

Harvey Kellogg, founder of Kellogg's Cereals

I am on the verge of 85.... I have lived quite long enough and I am trying to die; but I simply cannot do it. A single beef steak would finish me; but I cannot bring myself to swallow it. I am oppressed with a dread of living forever. That is the only disadvantage of vegetarianism.

George Bernard Shaw, playwright

World Hunger

Feeding the earth's people is... a political and economic problem which you and I must help to solve.

Frances Moore Lappé, author

What makes more sense: using land to grow grains and vegetables to feed billions of people, or using the land to raise animals as food that only a small part of the world's population can afford to buy? For people who care about human rights, the answer is obvious. As they see it, using land to raise plant crops is not only a more efficient way to feed people, it's also the right thing to do.

Rachel, 12: *I was helping my school raise money for famine relief, and I found out two amazing things. One was that hundreds of millions of people — nearly one-quarter of the world's population — go hungry. The second was* *that if all the land being used to raise animals was used to grow grains and vegetables instead, everybody in the world could be fed. That made me mad. Imagine, all those people starving, just because of the way land is used! Then I realized I could do something about it. My not eating meat obviously doesn't feed the masses, but it's a small way I can make a difference.*

Did You Know?

- Almost 40 per cent of the world's grain production is fed to animals. In the United States, it's 70 per cent.
- It takes 7 pounds (3.18 kg) of grain to produce 1 pound (.45 kg) of pork, 5 pounds (2.27 kg) of grain to produce 1 pound (.45 kg) of beef, and 3 pounds (1.36 kg) of grain to produce 1 pound (.45 kg) of chicken.
- A steer grazing on an acre of grass will produce enough meat to feed one person for 77 days. But, planted with soybeans, that same acre will produce enough food to feed the person for 2200 days.

What did the cow say when the farmer decided to become a vegetarian?

That's moo-sic to my ears.

Try This

Find a person who weighs about 250 pounds (113 kg). That's how much meat the average American eats in a year. Now find something that weighs 5 pounds (2.2 kg) – say, a small sack of flour. That's how much meat is eaten in a year by the average person in India.

Many things made me become a vegetarian — among them, the higher food yield as a solution to world hunger.

John Denver, musician

17

Religion

For many kids, being a vegetarian isn't a lifestyle choice, it's a spiritual practice. Some religious groups refrain from eating meat so as not to kill. Others believe in taking a peaceful, nonviolent approach to life.

Geeta, 9: I'm a Hindu, and we believe that all life forms have consciousness. We try to follow the path of ahimsa, or nonviolence. So we don't believe in killing animals for food, because that would be an act of violence and cruelty toward another living thing. The way Hindus see it, you can't eat meat and live a peaceful life.

Good Taste

Some kids start the journey to a meatless way of life for the simplest reason of all: just plain fun.

Luke, 14: I really had no intention of becoming a vegetarian. But one of my buddies made vegetarian lasagna for a party one time. Man, that was good! It was full of veggies, and I didn't even miss the meat. I thought, "I should try more of this stuff." Before I knew it I was getting into all this great vegetarian food and eating less and less meat. I'm not a total vegetarian but I'm getting there.

Try This

You've heard from other kids. Now it's your turn. Grab a sheet of paper and list your top three reasons for being a vegetarian. Ask your vegetarian friends to do the same. Were you and your friends motivated by the same things, or did you have different reasons?

Hey! You're in Good Company!

More people than you might think are vegetarians – movie stars, Olympic athletes, rock musicians, and the person next door. Here's a sampling of famous vegetarians from different walks of life.

Vegetarian Entertainers

Bryan Adams
Fiona Apple
Drew Barrymore
David Bowie
Elvis Costello
Dr. Dre
David Duchovny
Melissa Etheridge
Michael Jackson
Lenny Kravitz
Paul McCartney
Natalie Merchant
Moby
Gwyneth Paltrow
Monica Potter
Raffi
Julia Stiles
Liv Tyler
Shania Twain
Vanessa Williams

Vegetarian Athletes

Hank Aaron, baseball player
Billie Jean King, tennis player
Killer Kowalski, wrestler
Carl Lewis, Olympic track athlete
Edwin Moses, Olympic hurdler
Martina Navratilova, tennis player
Dave Scott, Ironman triathlon athlete
Bill Walton, basketball player

Vegetarian Scientists, Philosophers, and Political Leaders

Buddha
Charles Darwin
Thomas Edison
Albert Einstein
Mohandas Gandhi
Sir Isaac Newton
Plato
Pythagoras
Albert Schweitzer
Socrates

Vegetarian Writers and Artists

Louisa May Alcott
Leonardo da Vinci
George Bernard Shaw
Isaac Bashevis Singer
Leo Tolstoy
Vincent van Gogh
H.G. Wells

Convincing Parents...
and Other Sticky Situations

What do I do if my parents freak out when I tell them I want to be a vegetarian? How do I persuade my friends that I haven't gone off the deep end? How do I cope with holiday dinners, when the entire family – except me – is digging into the roast? What do I do about birthday parties at McDonald's, school cafeterias with no meatless options, dinner at my best friend's house when I'm handed a big juicy steak...? H-E-L-P!

Relax. Help is at hand. Other vegetarian kids have been there. Here, they share their experiences, which can help you survive the tricky situations you're bound to face, both as a vegetarian and as a young adult. After all, as you grow up, you'll be making more decisions about your own health and your own life – decisions that your parents and others may have a hard time accepting. So any skills that can help you demonstrate that your choice is well thought-out and worthy of respect are bound to come in handy!

Myths and Misconceptions

When you announce to friends and family that you're going vegetarian, you're likely to be met with "Isn't it dangerous?" and "Won't you be bored eating the same thing all the time?" That's because most people don't understand what vegetarianism is all about.

"Vegetarians don't get enough protein."

They do so – as long as they eat a varied diet that meets healthy food-group requirements. And you'll find out exactly how to do that in this book. Besides, most meat-eating North Americans get too much protein, which can lead to kidney disease and osteoporosis.

"Vegetarians don't get enough iron."

They do so – as long as they eat a varied diet. Oops! Already said that. But it's true. And you'll learn which foods are high in iron, as well as an iron-plus-vitamin-C trick for absorbing more iron.

"Vegetarians don't get enough calcium."

They do so – as long as... you know the drill. What's more, vegetarians and vegans are likely to absorb more calcium from their food than meat-eaters are, because too much protein prevents the body from absorbing calcium.

"Vegetarians suffer from a vitamin B$_{12}$ deficiency."

Not necessarily. A B$_{12}$ deficiency is rare even among vegans – probably because they're generally careful about getting enough. And you'll find out how to avoid that problem in later in this book.

"Vegetarians have no energy and get sick a lot."
Try telling that to tennis champion Billie Jean King. Or Dave Scott, multiple winner of the Ironman triathlon. Or the mountain-trekking sherpas of the Himalayas. Vegetarians all. So there goes the "no energy" argument. As for getting sick, the opposite is true. Vegetarians typically have lower rates of heart disease and some types of cancer than meat-eaters do.

"Vegetarianism is a hassle. You need to figure out how to combine proteins, and it takes forever to cook those finicky vegetarian meals."
Nonsense. You don't need to calculate the protein balance of every meal, as long as you eat a variety of proteins throughout the day. And what sounds quicker and easier – whipping up a veggie stir-fry or cooking the Sunday roast?

"Vegetarians live on tofu, granola, and seaweed."
Yeah, and yams, kidney beans, oranges, cauliflower, chick peas, cashews, linguini, potatoes, lentils, pizza, strawberries...

"Vegetarians don't eat a balanced diet."
A recent study reported by *Vegetarian Times* magazine shows that, on any given day, the average American doesn't eat a single vegetable. And that, of those who do eat at least one vegetable, most eat only potatoes. So who doesn't eat a balanced diet?

"Vegetarians can't eat out."
Baloney (pardon the expression!). More and more restaurants have vegetarian dishes on their menus; some fast-food places even offer meatless options. And there is the wealth of ethnic restaurants that feature vegetarian cuisine.

"Kids use vegetarianism as a excuse to get super-thin."
Yes, there is a small percentage of teens who are obsessed with being thin, and some mistakenly think that cutting out meat is the answer. But the good news is that most vegetarian kids are healthy and normal, and they approach vegetarianism for the right reasons – to be even healthier and to live well on the planet.

"Vegetarianism is all right for adults, but kids need meat to grow properly."
A varied balanced meat-free diet is safe for vegetarian and vegan kids, and professional dietitians say so.

Frequently Asked Questions

Here's where our resident vegetarian guru, Veggie Dude, gives you the lowdown on the questions you've been dying to ask.

Q: Dear Veggie Dude,
What if I miss meat?
Cravin'

A: Dear Cravin',
Chill out, buddy! It's natural, especially at first. If you give in a few times, you're not going to be hauled up before a firing squad. But if you keep drooling over steaks and ribs, maybe you're not cut out to be a vegetarian. That's cool. Even if you eat less meat, that's a positive step.
Veggie Dude

Q: Dear Veggie Dude,
If I'm a vegetarian, does that mean I'm organic, too?
Confused

A: Dear Confused,
Not necessarily. "Vegetarian" is about what foods you eat,

"organic" is about how food is grown. Organic means that food has been grown without artificial fertilizers and pesticides and all that junk. Organic food is generally considered healthier than food that's been sprayed with chemicals, and it's certainly better for the environment. Usually costs more, though. Many vegetarians prefer to buy organic food, but it's your call.

Veggie Dude

Q: Dear Veggie Dude,

Is it better to go vegetarian a little at a time or all at once?

Torn

A: Dear Torn,

No worries! There's no right way or wrong way. Some kids prefer to cut out meat "cold turkey." (Very punny!) Others find it easier to gradually reduce the amount of meat they eat or cut out one type of meat at a time.

Veggie Dude

Q: Dear Veggie Dude,

I don't know any other vegetarian kids. How can I find someone to talk to?

Lonely

A: Dear Lonely,

Hey, kiddo, you're not alone. The Vegetarian Youth Network and other websites offer on-line vegetarian pen pals and chat groups (for addresses, see the "Off You Go!" section of this book). Also, talk to your friends. Although they may not be vegetarians, they may dig your reasons for being one – you may be more in sync than you think.

Veggie Dude

Q: Dear Veggie Dude,

How do I decide whether to be a vegetarian or a vegan?

Waffling

A: Dear Waffling,

Don't sweat it. One isn't more "right" than the other. It depends on what you're into. If animal welfare is your thing, you may want to go all the way and totally get off animal products. If it's more about personal health, just giving up meat may be enough of a change. One thing, though – to be a healthy vegan, you need to stay on top of nutrition more, so you might be better off starting out as a vegetarian and working your way from there.

Veggie Dude

Q: Dear Veggie Dude,

If I wear leather shoes, does that mean I'm not a true vegetarian?

Shoeless

A: Dear Shoeless,

No, it doesn't, though it does mean you're not a vegan. Leather is a tough one. (Get it? Tough one? Hah!) It's true that leather shoes (and jackets and purses) are made from hides left after animals are slaughtered, so if you buy leather shoes, you're indirectly supporting the meat industry. But other options have problems, too. Cloth shoes get soaked (wet feet!), plastic shoes don't breathe well (stinky feet!), and non-leather shoes usually don't last as long as leather ones, so they have to be replaced more often (expensive feet!). The choice is yours. But remember – even if you do wear leather, as a vegetarian you're still helping animals. And for goodness sake, get some shoes on!

Veggie Dude

Convincing Your Parents

"You're *what*!"

"You'll get sick and die!"

"I'm not cooking you special meals."

"Does that mean you've joined a cult?"

Your parents may be totally supportive when you tell them you're going vegetarian. Or they might freak out with reactions like the ones above. Why? They may think that your decision will mean more work for them. They may feel that you're not just rejecting their diet, you're rejecting them and everything they stand for. They may be afraid that you're endangering your health.

These reactions aren't surprising, when you think about it. Your parents love you and are concerned about you. Naturally, they're suspicious of anything they think poses a threat to your well-being, whether it's your diet or your career choice or your hair color. And sometimes it's hard for parents to let go and admit that their kids are ready to make some big decisions for themselves.

At the same time, you've given this move a lot of thought, and you want to be taken seriously. So, how do you win your parents over?

Be prepared.

Know your nutritional information and show your parents how your diet will provide all the nutrients you need. Outline sample menus and show how they add up to a healthy diet. Sometimes this reassurance is all it takes to dismiss parents' fears.

Carolynne, 17: My parents urged me to talk to a doctor, so, to put their minds at rest, I did. And I was glad, because I found out what I needed to eat — and my parents got off my back.

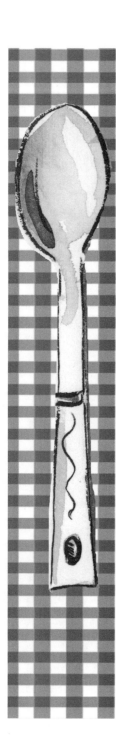

Be rational.

Explain your reasons without getting overwrought. Just as you don't want your parents to put down your dietary choice, don't put down theirs.

Be ready to compromise.

Remember: independence doesn't come overnight, but in small steps that both sides can live with.

Brianna, 11: When I first became a vegetarian, I didn't want to eat eggs or dairy, but my parents were really worried, so I agreed to eat eggs. They're still trying to get me to eat fish, though!

Be reassuring.

Make sure your parents know that your choice won't mean hours of extra work for them. And back up your words by helping out with the shopping and cooking.

Be patient.

It can take parents a long time to accept a decision they don't understand or agree with. Most come around when they see that their children are healthy (maybe even healthier than before) and when they realize that the family is not saddled with extra work or expense, that this new diet is not weird, that it's not "just a phase" but a lifestyle choice their kids are committed to. Sometimes a child's decision to go vegetarian inspires the rest of the family to eat less meat and try new foods. So, in the end, your parents may thank you!

Megan, 22: My folks were totally behind me when I became a vegetarian. But when I told them I was becoming a vegan, they were upset. They thought it was extreme and I'd get sick. Now that it's been a few years, and they understand more about veganism and see that I'm okay, they're more supportive. But my mom still has reservations and I know she'd like to see me eat eggs and dairy. There's still a bit of pressure. That's just something I have to live with.

Winning Over Your Friends

Picture this scenario: After a movie, you and your friends stop at the local greasy spoon. Instead of the usual burger and fries, you order a salad. "What's up with that?" your friends want to know. "Well... I've been meaning to tell you..." you say, "I've given up meat." Their reaction is:

❏ laughter

❏ shock

❏ pity

❏ all of the above

Friends don't usually freak out the way parents do, but they may still react negatively. Why? They may not understand what vegetarianism is all about and think it's weird. They may feel you're judging them and putting them down. They may be afraid you'll be no fun anymore – not able to go out for a snack, always obsessing about food, trying to foist strange soy products on them.

Whether you're switching to vegetarianism or making some other lifestyle change, you still need to keep them on your side. How?

Be straight with them.
Answer questions honestly and directly. Sometimes, just understanding where you're coming from is enough to persuade friends that your new meatless regime is okay.

Be tolerant.
No one likes to be reminded that they're eating something that used to have eyes. Just do your thing – with dignity but without

preaching. When they see that you're focusing on how *you* eat, not judging how *they* eat, they'll relax.

Carolynne, 17: When I told my friends I was becoming a vegetarian, some of them thought it was crazy. They said, "Cows are here to be eaten." I could have argued, but instead I said, "Well, I guess that's your opinion. I have my own opinion. We can agree to disagree." And we left it at that.

Be fun.

Introduce your friends to new vegetarian foods at your birthday party, on a picnic, or at a class pot-luck, so they can see what your new diet is all about. But don't force new foods on them or lecture them about how healthy the dish is. Let good tastes win them over.

Leanne, 15: It helps to have a sense of humor. Some of my friends wave their hamburgers under my nose and say, "Oooh, this is so good!" I just laugh.

Of course, some friends will support you, no questions asked. You may even find some new buddies.

Megan, 22: When I became a vegan, none of my close friends ate meat but no one was a hard-core vegan either. I was sort of lonely. So I put up posters around school: "Vegan seeks like-minded people to share food and recipes" — and people began getting in touch. One guy has turned out to be one of my best friends.

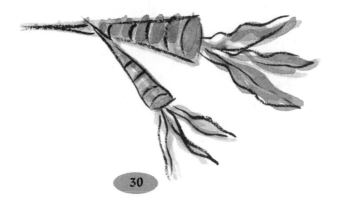

More Sticky Situations
Family Holiday Dinners

Thanksgiving turkey, Easter ham, Passover chicken, Chinese New Year's pork – whatever your heritage, chances are holiday dinners revolve around meat. And the meat dish may symbolize more than just food. It may represent generations of family tradition. It may even have religious significance. So when you refuse to eat Aunt Millie's marvelous meatballs or Grandma's famous holiday ham, you're not just hurting the cook's feelings, you appear to be turning your back on the entire history and culture of your family! How do you handle this sensitive situation?

Be ready to explain your reasons.
This may be the first time your relatives have been faced with vegetarianism, and they may be at a loss to understand why someone would willingly give up what they see as the most important part of the meal. Be patient, respectful, and clear.

Be tactful.
Reassure the chef that it's nothing personal, and prove it by eating everything else he or she cooked. It may take several dinners, but eventually Grandma and Aunt Millie will stop taking your refusal as an insult.

Be prepared to face pressure – and to stick to your guns.
Eventually your relatives will realize you mean it, and will stop trying to get you to eat meat.

Leanne, 15: At family dinners, someone always says, "Just have a slice of turkey, come on, just one slice." But I just brush it off.

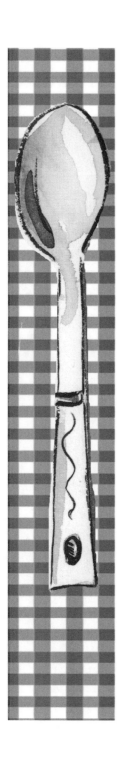

Be creative.

Offer to bring a vegetarian dish. That way, at least you'll have a main course to eat – and maybe some of your relatives will get turned on to veggie fare! If turkey stuffing is on the menu, ask the chef to leave some out before it goes into the bird. Then you can make your own stuffing with vegetarian seasonings and bake it separately. And remember to eat all the side dishes. At holiday dinners, there are usually so many salads, vegetables, bread, and casseroles, you're in no danger of starving.

Restaurants

Much depends on whether you're going to a fine restaurant or a fast-food joint. Most better restaurants have at least one vegetarian option, but it's best to call ahead and let the restaurant know you're a vegetarian, so they're prepared. Once you're there, tell your server that you're a vegetarian and ask for suggestions. Often, the chef is willing to adapt one of the meat-based dishes or even prepare a special meal.

Tracey, 17: If there're no vegetarian entreés on the menu, I go with a combination of appetizers, soups, and salads. Sometimes that makes a great meal.

Things aren't as easy at fast-food restaurants where the meals are pre-set and the choices more limited. Still, many fast-food restaurants have salads and potatoes, and sometimes you can get vegetarian burritos or pizzas.

Most restaurants have comment cards, so fill them out or write to the company to request more vegetarian options. And urge other people to do the same. The more people restaurants hear from, the more likely they'll be to pay attention.

Dinner at a Friend's House

The dilemma: do you tell your friend's parents you're a vegetarian ahead of time and hope they'll offer you something other than meat, or keep your mouth shut and work with whatever's being served? It depends on what you're comfortable with.

Tim, 13: I don't like to make anybody go to any trouble, so I usually don't say anything. I just skip the meat and heap on the side dishes. Sometimes my friend's mom notices and offers me cheese or peanut butter or something. If it's not a lot of work, I say okay.

Andrea, 16: I don't like to make my friends' parents feel bad by refusing to eat what they're serving, so I usually tell them ahead of time that I don't eat meat. I feel funny being pushy, but it saves embarrassment on both sides. And at least I get something to eat!

One solution is to offer to bring a vegetarian dish. Or you can ask to fix yourself a sandwich. Most friends' parents won't be insulted – they'd rather see you eat *something* than go hungry out of fear of offending them.

Carolynne, 17: Once when I was babysitting, the little girl I was looking after decided to do something nice for me and made me a ham sandwich. It was really awkward and I didn't know what to say. So I waited for her to leave the room and then wrapped it up and stuck it back in the fridge!

School Cafeterias

If your school cafeteria serves food, chances are the choices range from meatloaf to fish sticks. Want to get meatless options on the menu? Don't complain – do something!

First, talk to other kids in the school and make sure that there's a demand for vegetarian fare. After all, you can't expect the

33

cafeteria to change the menu for just one or two people. You might want to round up a team of buddies to help – in addition to sharing the work, it'll show the school that there's real interest.

Once you've confirmed the demand, set up a meeting with the cafeteria director and the principal. Show them what you found when you talked to the other students. Present information about what vegetarianism is and the benefits of a vegetarian diet. Have some recipes on hand – choose ones that are relatively simple to make and that you think most people will like.

Above all, be positive. Make it clear that you're ready to help, whether by providing recipes, taste-testing vegetarian dishes, or surveying fellow students on different vegetarian options. If your cafeteria does adopt a vegetarian dish, show your appreciation. Make sure you and your friends buy it. Thank the cafeteria director and the school administration, and encourage others to give them positive feedback.

For more information, contact EarthSave (see the "Off You Go!" section of this book) and ask for their *Healthy School Lunch Action Guide,* a handbook designed to help students work for healthier school food choices.

Away From Home
Air Travel
Most airlines provide vegetarian meals on request, and some even offer variations such as lacto-ovo or vegan. Ask for a vegetarian meal when you make your reservation, and confirm the request when you check in. You might not get much more than frozen vegetables and noodles, but at least you won't have to pick around the meat.

Summer Camp

With increasing numbers of vegetarian kids, many camps offer vegetarian meal plans, or at least meatless options along with the regular fare. But don't count on it – call ahead to find out what kind of food will be served. You may need to bring your own supply of vegetarian foods and arrange to have special meals prepared, either by you or by camp staff.

On the Road

You're in a strange town and all you see are burger joints. What to do? Look in the Yellow Pages for natural foods or ethnic restaurants. If that doesn't turn up anything, ask at the local health-food store. Before you leave home, check out websites for vegetarian restaurants where you'll be traveling. And don't forget to pack the *Vegetarian Journal's Guide to Natural Foods Restaurants in the U.S. and Canada* and *Vegetarian Handbook: a new guide to eating healthy across Canada* (for ordering information, see the "Off You Go!" section of this book).

Camping

Good news! Vegetarianism and camping are a natural match. Vegetarian foods are light, easy to pack, nutritious, and filling. And just think – the more you eat, the lighter your pack gets! Here are some suggestions for food to trek with:

- Quick-cooking whole grains such as rice, millet, and couscous
- Pasta
- Quicker-cooking legumes such as lentils and textured vegetable protein (TVP)
- Nuts and seeds, either on their own or in trail mixes
- Granola, muesli, or homemade pancake mix
- Nutritional yeast to sprinkle on food for added flavor and B vitamins

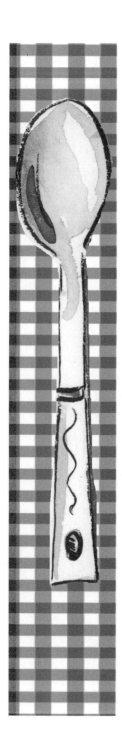

◆ Powdered dairy milk (some health-food stores may carry powdered soy milk)

Snappy Comebacks

Let's face it – sometimes a dumb question deserves a smart answer. Especially if it's an off-the-wall question about vegetarianism!

Q: You're a vegetarian? Does that mean you've changed your religion?

Yeah, it's the new Worldwide Vegetarian Faith, and I'm the High Priest/Priestess!

Q: Don't you get sick of eating rabbit food all the time?

Yeah, but it's worth it to have this cute little bushy tail.

Q: How many vitamin pills do
you have to take every day?

*Four hundred seventy-six.
But it only takes three hours
to swallow them all.*

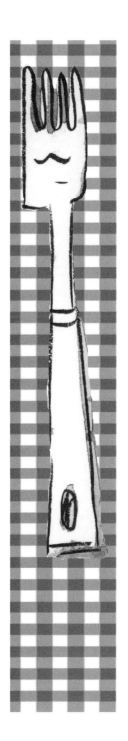

Q: Plants have feelings, don't they?
So why don't you give up plants, too?

*It's my way of preventing the
world from getting completely
overrun with wild vegetables.*

Food, Glorious Food!

Have you ever taken a really close look at the food you eat? Where did the tofu in your stir-fry come from? How did potatoes get to be one of the most popular vegetables in the world? Who invented peanut butter? What vegetarian foods might come along in the future?

Here you'll find the answers to those questions. But first, a brief look at vegetarianism – how it started and grew into the movement it is today.

A Short History of Vegetarianism

Prehistoric time

Although we often think of prehistoric people as bloodthirsty carnivores, they weren't. Our early ancestors lived on a semi-vegetarian diet made up mostly of nuts, seeds, fruits, and vegetables, along with a small amount of meat.

2000 BC–600 AD: Ancient Greece

The philosopher Pythagoras (born 580 BC) is considered the Father of Vegetarianism. He believed that animals have souls with equal worth to those of humans, so animals should not be killed and eaten. Whether because they agreed or just couldn't afford meat, ordinary Greeks ate a vegetarian diet. A typical meal consisted of flat barley bread, salad, cheese, olives, and figs, washed down with wine.

300 BC–400 AD: Ancient Rome

Suffering from an illness? Take some butter. Need to clear up your complexion? Splash milk on your skin. That's what the ancient Romans did. Too bad they didn't use the butter and milk to liven up their diet, which largely consisted of flat hard barley bread and a thick soup of barley and beans.

1000–4000 AD: The Middle Ages

As the Roman Empire fell, Christianity spread across Europe. Arguing the opposite view from Pythagoras, Christian thinkers said that animals were placed on earth for the use of humans – so we were justified in killing and eating them. Not surprisingly, vegetarianism went into decline.

1300–1600: The Renaissance

As in earlier centuries, the poor ate mostly grains and vegetables, while their wealthy lords feasted on meat. The Italian painter Leonardo da Vinci (1452-1519), a vegetarian, called meat-eating "murder." But most people went on eating meat anyway.

16th to 18th Centuries: The Age of Exploration

Foods went on a global journey. European explorers brought potatoes, peanuts, kidney beans, pineapples, peppers, and tomatoes from the Americas back home to Europe and to their colonies in Asia and Africa. And they carried African yams, sweet potatoes, lima beans, and chili peppers to Asia, Europe, and the Americas.

1847

Members of the Bible Christian Church, led by William Cowherd (unfortunate name!), founded the Vegetarian Society, the first vegetarian organization in the western world – a group that is still active today.

Feeling Frisky

Most people think that the word "vegetarian" comes from "vegetable." Wrong! The Vegetarian Society coined the term from the Latin word vegetus, meaning lively or vigorous, to describe how their diet made them feel.

Late 1800s

Vegetarian foods were advertised as health boosters. In 1898, Dr. Kellogg of Michigan promoted his new product, corn flakes, as a vegetarian health food.

1908

The International Vegetarian Union – the world's first international vegetarian group – was formed. Nearly one hundred years later, this organization is still going strong.

1960s–1970s
Vegetarianism enjoyed a surge of popularity as people became more aware of the importance of eating well to stay healthy, interested in Eastern religions and their teachings about the sacredness of all life, and concerned about the environment.

1980s
Television images of starving children in famine-stricken countries heightened concerns about world hunger and farming practices.

Early 1990s
New nutritional information confirmed that a healthy vegetarian diet was easier to achieve than previously thought.

Late 1990s
Incidents of water contamination from manure and outbreaks of meat-borne diseases such as "mad cow disease" raised questions about the safety of livestock agriculture.

Today
Vegetarianism is more popular than ever!

The Vegetarian Foods Hall of Fame

When is food more than food? When it's also history, folklore, botany, nutrition, trade, mythology, exploration, war... Introducing the stories behind some of the most important vegetarian foods in the world.

Soybeans

Often called "the meat without bones," soybeans are the champions of the bean world.

- Soybeans contain three times as much protein as wheat or corn, more fiber and minerals than other beans, and most of the B vitamins.
- They help the body fight infection and retain bone mass, prevent certain types of cancer, and lower cholesterol levels.
- In addition to food, they provide oil, soap, diesel fuel, glue, and plastic.

The ancient Chinese knew a good thing when they saw one. Around 2700 BC, the emperor Shen Nung named soybeans one of five "sacred foods," along with rice, millet, wheat, and barley. Chinese Buddhist monks, who were vegetarians, introduced soybeans to Korea and Japan between 200 BC and 200 AD.

Christian missionaries brought soybeans from China to Europe in the early 1700s, but at first they were grown only for decoration, not for food. When American farmers began to grow soybeans, about a century later, they mainly used them for animal feed, although soldiers in the Civil War made a coffee substitute from them. After World War II, soybeans became a major crop in the American midwest, and today the U.S. is the world's biggest grower, producing half of all soybeans grown worldwide.

Soy-mobile

American auto-maker Henry Ford had a passion for soybeans. Not only did he eat them, he also created auto parts from soybean plastic. One of Ford's cars sported gearshift knobs, window frames, pedals, and an exterior made from soybeans!

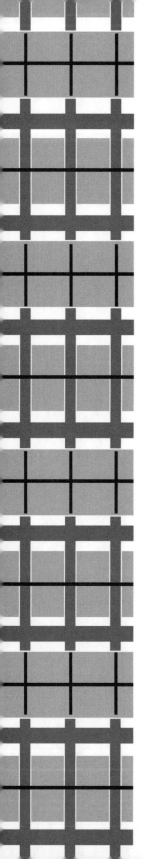

Soybeans are legumes, which means that their seeds grow in pods. Like all legumes, soybeans form nodules on their roots that absorb nitrogen from the air. Since crops need nitrogen to grow, soy plants, plowed back into the soil after the beans have been harvested, make an excellent fertilizer.

There's only one problem with these incredible beans: they're hard to digest. So most people eat soybeans after they have been made into other foods, such as tofu, tempeh, and miso.

Tofu

Legend has it that, during the Chinese Tang dynasty (618–907 AD), a public official was so honest that he refused to take bribes. As a result, he was too poor to buy meat. So, to feed his family, he invented tofu. To this day, some Chinese call honest government officials "tofu officials."

Known as "the cow of China," tofu's protein is similar in quality to that of meat. But tofu is really more like cheese in the way it is made. Soy milk (see below) is thickened with a mineral salt, forming curds – that's why tofu's other popular name is "bean curd." Curds that are left unpressed become the soft or silken tofu used in beverages, salad dressings, and baking; pressed curds form firm blocks that are ideal for stir-frying, grilling, and broiling.

The bad thing about tofu is that it's bland. The good thing about tofu is that it picks up whatever flavorings and seasonings it's mixed with. That makes tofu one of the most versatile foods around, and explains why it shows up in everything from gingery stir-fries to fiery chilis to sweet desserts.

Soy Milk and Soy Milk Products

Soy milk isn't really milk, but is made from cooked soybeans. It can be used in exactly the same ways as dairy milk – as a drink, over cereal, in smoothies. Most brands are now fortified with calcium, vitamin D, and other nutrients. Soy cheese, soy yogurt, soy ice cream, and soy sour cream are also available.

Tempeh

Fermented soybeans don't sound very appetizing, do they? But when they're tempeh (say "*tem*-pay"), they're delicious. Tempeh is made from fermented soybeans formed into cakes or chunks. Firmer than tofu and with a tangy flavor, tempeh can be grilled, added to soups and stews, or sautéed in stir-fries.

Miso

Miso (say "*mee*-so") is a paste of fermented soybeans. Rich and salty, it's used to season soups, sauces, and gravies.

Soy Sauce

Hard to imagine eating Chinese food without soy sauce, isn't it? This salty flavoring is brewed from roasted soybeans and wheat. Tamari (say "tah-*mah*-ree") is a natural soy sauce brewed using a traditional Japanese method.

Textured Vegetable Protein (TVP)

TVP is made from soy flour and comes in dried granules, flakes, or chunks. TVP plumps up in only a few minutes when you add boiling water, providing a protein-rich meat-like addition to casseroles, chilis, and veggie patties.

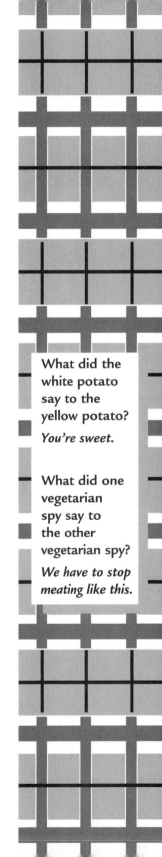

What did the white potato say to the yellow potato?

You're sweet.

What did one vegetarian spy say to the other vegetarian spy?

We have to stop meating like this.

Around the World with Soy Foods

China: In Moo Shu Tempeh, a spicy tempeh mixture is rolled up inside pancakes.

Malaysia: Taubu goreng is tofu cakes served with peanut sauce.

Japan: The Japanese are so fond of miso soup, they eat it almost every day.

Lentils

What comes in shades of orange, pink, green, yellow, and brown, cooks in about 45 minutes, and has been known throughout the ages as "poor man's food"? The lentil, of course.

Lentils are a legume. They're also a pulse. What's the difference? Legumes are plants that form their seeds in pods. Pulses are the actual seeds of legumes. A dry land crop, lentils need some rainfall but don't require irrigation. They thrive in places like India, which produces 800,000 tons of lentils a year, half of the world's supply.

Lentils are among the world's oldest cultivated foods. In Iraq, archeologists have found seeds dating back 9000 years. Lentils were also grown in ancient Greece, Egypt, and Rome. Because they are easy to grow and cheap, lentils have long been a staple food of the poor.

All that changed during the reign of the French King Louis XV (1715-1774). He named them "lentilles à la reine" (queen's lentils) after his wife, which made them popular throughout France. From there, lentils accompanied explorers and missionaries to Canada. A French priest, Father St. John, planted lentils with the Iroquois Indians in the St. Lawrence River valley. By the late 1700s, lentils had made their way down to America, where Thomas Jefferson grew them on his Virginia estate.

Why all the fuss over a small nondescript seed? Lentils are among the most nutritious and easy-to-digest legumes. They're loaded with fiber, protein, iron, and other vitamins and minerals. And they're easy to cook.

Around the World with Lentils

Armenia: Lentil soup includes apricots and eggplants.
India: Dal is a puree of lentils and spices, served with almost every meal.
Ethiopia: Yesmesirkik is a stew of lentils and 12 different spices.
Italy: Pastitsio is a pasta dish featuring lentils, eggplant, tomatoes, noodles, and cheese.

Quinoa

If you've ever been sent out to the garden to pull weeds, you're familiar with a relative of quinoa (say "*keen*-wah"). Quinoa is the grain of a plant in the pigweed family. Although gardeners may not like it, vegetarians and nutritionists do. Quinoa contains more protein than any other grain. In fact, the quality of its protein is similar to that of milk. Quinoa also provides carbohydrates, fiber, oil, calcium, iron, and several vitamins. It's light, tasty, and easy to digest, too.

Quinoa is not nearly as well known in North America as it is in its native South America, where it has been grown since at least 3000 BC. In the 1400s and 1500s AD, quinoa was cultivated by the Incas of Peru, who called it "the mother grain" and revered it as sacred. Along with corn and potatoes, quinoa was one of three staple foods of the Incas, and even today most of the world's crop is grown by Aymara and Quechua Indians in mountainous regions of Peru, Ecuador, Bolivia, Colombia, Argentina, and Chile.

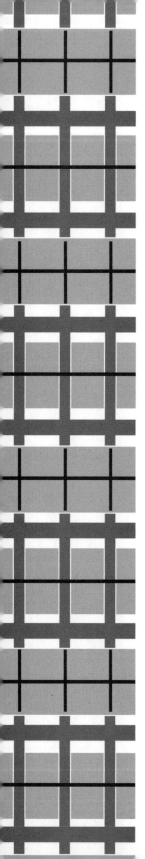

When the Spanish invaded South America in the 1500s, they discouraged the cultivation of quinoa – possibly to make the Incas easier to conquer – and its production declined. Still, quinoa hung on in the Andes, where local people grew it for their own use. Eventually, North Americans discovered its fine flavor and nutritional benefits, and today there is a small but thriving quinoa industry in North America.

Not a Scrap Left

The entire quinoa plant can be put to use. The grain is cooked like rice or ground into flour for bread and biscuits; the leaves are eaten as a vegetable or fed to animals; and the stalks can be burned as fuel.

The quinoa plant produces a small seed that looks like a cross between a sesame seed and a millet grain. Before washing, the seed may be red, purple, blue-black, orange, or pink; after washing, it's usually pale yellow. With its light texture and slightly nutty flavor, quinoa can be used in any recipe that calls for cooked grains. Substitute it for rice in stir-fries and pilafs, cook it as a nourishing breakfast pudding, toss it with vegetables and herbs in a cold salad, incorporate it into casseroles, tuck it into wraps – the possibilities are almost endless.

Peanuts

It's not a pea. It's not a nut. It's a legume. And it's eaten all over the world. The peanut originated in South America, probably in Bolivia. Plants found in Brazil and the Caribbean islands date back 5000 years. Archeologists in Peru have found plazas littered with peanut shells, leading to speculation that people enjoyed them as a snack while watching an ancient version of a baseball game!

After Europeans invaded South America, it didn't take long for peanuts to make their way around the world. In the 1500s, Portuguese ships carried peanuts to west Africa; a century later, African slaves brought them back to North America. Southern plantation owners grew peanuts to feed pigs; later, people discovered that peanuts were tasty and nutritious, and began to raise them for human food.

During the American Civil War, soldiers in both armies were given rations of peanuts, which introduced Northerners to the "new" food. By the late 1880s, peanuts had become a popular snack throughout the U.S., eaten at sporting events and circuses. Today, peanuts are cultivated in more than 100 countries, with China and India growing most of the world's crop. Asians consume more peanuts than anyone else.

The Peanut Man

George Washington Carver, born a slave in the American South, became one of the most famous plant scientists in the world. In the early 1900s, he developed over 300 products made from peanuts, including shoe polish and shaving cream. Carver once served dinner guests a meal made entirely from peanuts, starting with peanut soup and finishing with peanut coffee!

Like other legumes, peanut plants fertilize the soil when they're plowed under. But that's not all the plant is good for. Ground peanut shells are used in everything from wallboard to kitty litter to fake fireplace logs. Peanut oil is made into soap, shaving cream, cosmetics, paint, and – *kaboom!* – explosives. But most people agree that the best use of peanuts is just plain munching. Picture a sack of peanuts in the shell, waiting to be cracked and eaten. Or a dish of roasted peanuts, full of salt and crunch. Can you eat just one? Dare you!

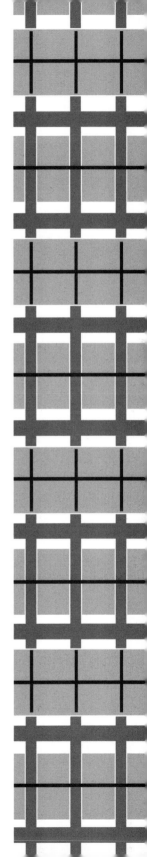

Around the World with Peanuts

Malaysia: Gado-gado is a spicy peanut sauce served over vegetables.

Mali: Kuli-kuli are fried peanut cakes.

North America: Peanut butter sandwiches, made with jam, jelly, honey, bananas, cheese, or pickles, are a staple of school lunches.

Potatoes

If you went back to 3000 BC, when potatoes were first grown in the mountainous Andes region of Peru, you probably wouldn't recognize the common spud. Early varieties came in sizes from as small as a walnut to as big as a grapefruit, and in shades of brown, red, orange, pink, purple, and black. The Incas called potatoes *papas* and ate them every day. But when the Spanish brought potatoes to Europe in the late 1500s, the new vegetable bombed. People didn't like its lumpy appearance and, because its rough skin reminded them of leprosy, they thought potatoes caused disease. So Europeans refused to eat them.

However, once people realized that potatoes were nutritious and easy to grow, they changed their minds. By the late 1600s, potatoes had become so important that, when Prussia was hit by crop failures and famine, King Frederick William decreed that peasants had to grow potatoes or they would have their noses and ears cut off! A Frenchman named Antoine Parmentier introduced potatoes into the court of King Louis XVI and Marie Antoinette, serving a royal meal of twenty potato dishes. So enamored were the French with the new vegetable that potato cultivation spread across Europe.

Nowhere was this more true than in Ireland. Early on, the Irish discovered that the potato was easy to grow and could feed a lot of people. This was important in a country of mostly poor landless folk, where one acre of potatoes could sustain a family of five for a year. By the early 1840s, almost half of Ireland's population, or nearly four million people, depended almost entirely on the potato for nourishment. In 1845, disaster struck. A disease attacked the Irish potato crop, potatoes rotted in the fields, and thousands of people died of starvation. The Irish Potato Famine lasted for four years. In that time, one and a half million people died, and the same number fled the country.

Today, Russia is the world's largest producer of potatoes, followed by China, Poland, and the U.S. Call them chips, fries, or spuds, enjoy them mashed, baked, boiled, or roasted, put them in soups, salads, pancakes, or pies – who doesn't love potatoes?

Around the World with Potatoes
Germany: Potato dumplings are served as a side dish or dropped into soup.
Ukraine: Perogies are filled with potatoes, onion, and cheese.
France: French fries – they were invented in the late 1700s.
Eastern Europe: Jewish cooks make potato latkes, or pancakes, which are fried and eaten with applesauce or sour cream.

Chick Peas

If you've ever dipped a piece of pita bread into a mound of garlicky hummus, you've eaten chick peas. This round, tan bean is a staple of Middle Eastern and South Asian cooking.

The chick pea's popularity isn't based only on its nutty buttery taste and its slightly crunchy texture. It's also due to its nutritional punch. The chick pea is high in protein, carbohydrates,

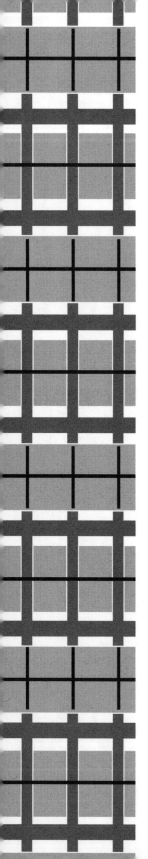

fiber, calcium, iron, and other minerals, and the fat it contains is the unsaturated, or "good" kind. Of all the legumes, the chick pea's protein is the easiest to digest. Chick peas provide a double-barreled health bonus: not only do they reduce cholesterol, but they also help to control diabetes.

> ## By Any Other Name...
> Chick peas are also known as garbanzos and ceci beans. In India, split chick peas are called chana dal and are sometimes used instead of split peas or lentils to make dal.

Chick peas originated around 6000 BC in the Fertile Crescent of the Near East. Today, they are the main legume grown and eaten in India – in fact, a whopping 90 per cent of world chick pea production is consumed there. The major producers are Turkey, Australia, Syria, Mexico, Argentina, the Canadian prairies, and the U.S.

Around the World with Chick Peas
Hummus: Popular throughout the Middle East, this spread is made from mashed chick peas, garlic, tahini (sesame paste), and lemon juice.
Falafel: These spicy chick pea balls are made from chick pea flour, water, and seasonings. In Israel and the Middle East, street-side falafel stands are as common as hot dog stands in North America.
Morocco: Chick peas are added to couscous for extra protein and crunch.

The Future of Food

Cast your mind into the future. What will food be like in twenty, fifty, one hundred years? Will we be growing food on distant planets? Will scientists be inventing new foods in the laboratory? Will we discover new uses for ancient plants? And how will all this affect vegetarianism and people's ability to eat healthful nutritious foods that protect the earth and its creatures?

Of course, no one knows. But we can speculate. These are some developments that we may see:

Genetically Modified Foods

You've probably heard about genetically modified (GM) foods. These are foods that have had genes belonging to other organisms added to them. The gene is the basic building block of heredity. In the seed of a pea plant, for instance, a gene tells the plant to grow to a certain size at a certain rate. In a fish, a gene helps the fish survive cold ocean waters. If you take the fish's cold water gene and transplant it into the pea, the pea plant may gain built-in "antifreeze" that allows it to survive colder temperatures.

The last several years have seen an explosion of GM plants – tomatoes that resist rotting, potatoes that are protected from insects and viruses, a type of rice that has a higher level of vitamin A than regular rice, soybeans and corn that can resist herbicides and pesticides so that farmers can spray to get rid of weeds and insects without harming the crop. Many people see great promise in GM plants to provide more, and better, food for humanity. But others have concerns about the safety of the new technology.

What does a vegetarian photographer say to get his subjects to smile?

"Soy 'Cheese!'"

GM Pros

- Since GM plants are resistant to insects and other pests, farmers can use less pesticide and herbicide, which is good for the environment.
- The nutritional value of foods is improved.
- Higher yields provide more food for hungry people and mean that less land is needed to grow crops.
- It's possible that genetic engineering could result in plants with built-in vaccines. That would help control disease, especially in developing countries that do not have adequate vaccination programs.

GM Cons

- We don't yet know the environmental impact of GM plants on insects, soil bacteria, and wildlife. By growing GM foods, we could be permanently altering ecosystems – not necessarily for the better.
- If GM foods are not clearly labeled, people might unwittingly eat something they're allergic to.
- Genetically engineered plants can spread if their pollens are carried by wind, insects, or birds. Already, GM canola plants have shown up in neighboring fields. Since they resist herbicides, they have become a weed that competes with the desired crop – and farmers can't get rid of them.
- Basically, eating GM foods is a huge human experiment. We don't know the long-term health effects of eating foods that contain the genes of species that we don't normally consume and aren't genetically programmed to eat.

Ocean Farming

The ocean floor is full of decayed animal and plant matter – in other words, it's rich in fertilizer. If that organic matter could be brought closer to the surface to take advantage of sunlight, we could grow food in rich ocean "fields."

Spirulina

Spirulina, or freshwater algae, contains 40 per cent more protein than meat. Currently, experiments are underway to grow spirulina in California and Mexico.

Space Stations

Perhaps someday we'll grow food on space stations. After all, there's plenty of solar power available, humans produce carbon dioxide (which plants need), and water and other elements could be extracted from human waste. You never know!

Be Smart – Stay Healthy

When you decided to become a vegetarian, one of your main reasons – perhaps your main reason – may have been to be healthier. And it's true that eating a vegetarian diet can make you feel great.

But simply going meat-free is no guarantee of health. To stay healthy, you've got to eat smart. Just as with any style of eating, a poorly balanced vegetarian diet can lead to health problems – some of them serious.

Soon we'll get down to the nuts and bolts – or is that nuts and beets? – of planning a healthy vegetarian diet that meets your nutritional needs. But first, let's go over some basic principles of healthy eating, and alert you to danger signs to watch out for.

Guidelines for Healthy Vegetarian Eating

Danger: Filling up on side dishes

If you just skip the meat and load up on potatoes, rice, bread, and salad, you won't be getting the nutrients you need. This could result in low energy and poor growth.

Smart Move: Think variety.

Reorganize your eating to include plenty of legumes, whole grains, fruits, vegetables, and milk or milk alternates every day. (To find out how to fit all of these foods into a healthy eating plan, see Food Groups for Vegetarians in the next chapter.) And try new foods once in a while. Quinoa? Tempeh? You never know – you might like it!

Danger: Replacing meat with too much dairy and eggs

Eggs and dairy products are good sources of protein and calcium, but they can also be high in fat. And relying on them too much means you're missing out on other nutrients. Replacing meat with milk, instead of with iron-rich legumes, can even result in an iron deficiency.

Smart Move: Replace meat with a mix of legumes, grains, nuts, seeds, and milk products.

And when it comes to dairy, think lower-fat. Most of the time, choose skim or low-fat milk, lower-fat cheeses, and low-fat or non-fat yogurt. Lower-fat ice creams or ice milks are also available. If you eat eggs, do so in moderation.

Danger: Loading up on junk food

Sure, we all crave a bag of potato chips or a chocolate bar once in a while. But if you're filling up on them you could be heading for trouble. For one thing, they're loaded with fat, sugar, and

salt – which, aside from causing health problems, aren't great for your waistline or your skin. For another, they take up space that nutritious foods should fill.

Smart Move: Go easy on junk.

When you do have snacks, make them count by choosing them from the recommended food groups. They'll help you meet your daily food requirements and they're healthier, too.

Danger: Filling up on refined grain products

White bread, white rice, white pasta... they'll fill you up, all right – with starch and not much more. That's because most of the nutritional goodness has been refined right out of them.

Smart Move: Choose whole grains most of the time.

That means choosing whole grain breads, cereals, and pastas, and eating brown rice instead of refined white rice. They're better for you than products made with refined grains or flours.

Danger: Skipping meals to lose weight

If you're trying to shed pounds, skipping breakfast or lunch can be tempting. But if you skip meals, you'll only be hungrier – and more likely to fill up on fattening junk food – later on.

Smart Move: Maintain a healthy weight by eating a balanced diet and exercising regularly.

Don't skip meals. Even if you're trying to lose weight. Especially if you're trying to lose weight. You need energy throughout the day. Instead of skipping meals, cut back on sweets and fatty foods, and try to be more active.

Step-by-Step Guide to Becoming a Vegetarian

There's no right way or wrong way to set out on a meatless path. But it does take planning and preparation. This checklist can get you started and help you succeed.

Do your homework.

Learn about nutrition. Find out what nutrients your body needs and where to find them. Make sure you know and understand the vegetarian food groups in the next chapter. Talk to other vegetarians. If you have questions or concerns, ask your family doctor or consult a professional dietitian.

Plan a week of menus.

Sample menus are included in the next chapter and in other books on being a vegetarian. You don't have to stick exactly to your menus but, if you plan ahead, you'll be prepared with healthy solutions when those hunger pangs strike.

Figure out who will cook.

Who does the cooking in your household? If special arrangements are needed to accommodate your diet, who will make them? You can't expect your parents to fix you separate meals. Be prepared to either cook for yourself or find ways to adapt the meals the rest of the family is eating.

Break it to your parents.

Be ready for their questions and objections. This is where you whip out your nutrition information and your carefully planned menus, and where you reassure them that your choice isn't going to disrupt the family's life. For pointers, see the chapter "Convincing Parents... and Other Sticky Situations."

Stock up on vegetarian foods.

Check the list of what to buy and where to buy it in the next chapter. But start out with small quantities until you find out what you like.

Experiment with vegetarian recipes.

This is the fun part. Try the recipes in this book. Check the terrific cookbooks listed in the "Off You Go!" section or at your local bookstore. Experiment and find out what you like.

Keep track of what you eat each day.

Check your totals against the recommended number of servings from the four food groups. This may sound like a lot of work, but it's the only way to be sure you're getting all the nutrients you need. After a while, the food guide will become second nature and you won't have to keep track anymore.

Try a new food at least once every few months.

Not just for fun but for health, too. The more varied your diet, the better your chances of getting well-balanced nutrition. Besides, you might discover a great new taste that you've been missing out on all your life!

Stay positive.

Your first few attempts at cooking may end up in the dog's dish. Or your family and friends may tease, criticize, or nag you. Or you may give in to a meat craving and scarf down a burger. Don't be hard on yourself. Becoming a vegetarian is a process, not an end result. Pick yourself up and try again.

Celebrate!

After a week, a month, or a year, give yourself a pat on the back. Rejoice in the fact that you're helping the planet, its animals, and your health. Have a party. Buy yourself a gift. Have a treat. Or simply look in the mirror and say, "Way to go!"

What You Can Do

Not content to simply cut meat from your diet? Get your friends organized and get involved! Here are ways that kids can make a difference:

◆ Write to your government representatives and urge them to support legislation that promotes environmental responsibility and the humane treatment of animals.

◆ Buy from companies that don't test their products on animals.

◆ Find a vegetarian pen pal in another country.

◆ Get your school cafeteria to offer meatless options.

- Join YES! or another environmentally friendly youth organizations. (See the "Off You Go!" section for names and addresses.)
- Lobby local fast-food restaurants to include vegetarian dishes on their menus.
- Start a vegetarian club to exchange recipes, shopping tips, nutrition information, etc.
- Make your lifestyle more "green": cycle or walk instead of asking for a ride, recycle, grow your own organic veggies, use cloth shopping bags, reduce the amount of packaging you buy and throw away, reuse scrap paper, wrap gifts in newspaper (comic strips are eye-catching!) instead of buying gift wrap.

Being a Vegetarian – It's Easier Than You Think

If you're a new vegetarian, you may be wondering what on earth to eat. Picture your pre-vegetarian dinner plate. It probably looked something like the meal shown on the facing page. Take away the meat, and you're left with side dishes. Boring! And not very nutritious, either.

What to do? The key is to remember that other v-word: VARIETY. There is a wealth of mouthwatering and nutritious foods to fill a vegetarian diet, from early-morning breakfast to midnight snacks, and from grab-as-you-go lunches to fun party treats. As a vegetarian, you can feast on fruits, vegetables, whole grain products, nuts, seeds, legumes, dairy products, and eggs. So forget about "doing without" meat. Re-think your plate. Think about what it could be full of instead of what it's missing. But first, let's review some nutritional basics.

Nutrition 101

It's simple. Your body needs carbohydrates, protein, fat, vitamins, and minerals. As long as you provide all of these nutrients in the right amounts, you'll grow properly, have enough energy, and stay healthy mentally and physically.

Carbohydrates

Carbohydrates are to your body what gasoline is to a car: They're the fuel that keeps your body going and gives you energy. Carbohydrates are found in grains (such as rice, wheat, oats, and barley), fruits and vegetables, legumes (dried beans and peas, such as lentils, chick peas, and kidney beans), seeds, and nuts. Everybody needs plenty of carbohydrates every day, but if you play sports or are very active, you need even more.

Fiber

Fiber is a type of complex carbohydrate that's found only in plant foods. It remains undigested when food enters the large intestine, and keeps our bodies – especially the digestive system – working properly. It also reduces the risk of heart disease and certain types of cancer, and helps control blood sugar to prevent diabetes. Fiber is abundant in foods vegetarians eat plenty of – legumes and whole grains.

Protein

Protein is the nutrient that helps your body grow and repair itself. If you're between the ages of 11 and 14, you need about 2 ounces (50 g) of protein a day. It's found in legumes, soy foods (such as tofu and tempeh), vegetables, grains, nuts, seeds, eggs, and dairy products.

Combining Proteins

Amino acids are the building blocks of protein, and certain amino acids need to be present in food for your body to use the protein. Nutritionists used to think you had to carefully combine proteins at each meal to make sure you were getting the right amino acids in the right amounts. But now we know that if you eat a balanced diet every day, with enough total calories and a variety of protein foods, you'll get all the amino acids and usable protein you need.

Fat

Wait a minute. Isn't everybody always telling us to eat less fat? Most of us could benefit from reducing the amount of fat in our diet. But the fact is that the body needs some fat to store energy and to help in the formation and function of healthy cells. The trick is to get the right kind of fat. There are saturated fats (the bad kind) and unsaturated fats (the good kind). And guess what – animal products, such as beef, bacon, and butter, contain saturated fat. But so do high-fat dairy products and hydrogenated oils (oils used in margarine and solid shortening). Even the "good" kind of fat – found in plant foods such as nuts and avocados – can be too much of a good thing. How to navigate through this slippery maze of fats? Eat them sparingly, avoid "bad" saturated fats, and, if you eat dairy, choose lower- fat products.

Good Fats

The fats that most people need more of are called omega-3 fatty acids. These essential fats are found in walnuts, canola oil, flaxseeds and flaxseed oil, hempseeds and hempseed oil, olives and olive oil.

Vitamins

Vitamin A

Think colors! This vitamin is found in yellow, orange, and dark green fruits and vegetables, as well as in fortified milk (dairy, soy, rice, and nut). It's important for night vision, healthy skin, and the development of strong bones and teeth.

B Vitamins

This family includes thiamin, riboflavin, niacin, vitamin B_6, folic acid, biotin, pantothenic acid, and choline. That's quite a mouthful! But the B vitamins do many important jobs in the body: they aid normal growth and appetite, release energy from food, help form red blood cells, help your nervous system and digestive system run properly, and keep your skin and eyes healthy. They're found in whole grains, vegetables, legumes, nuts, dairy products, and fortified foods, such as some breakfast cereals and pastas.

Vitamin B_{12}

You need only a tiny amount of this vitamin – two millionths of a gram a day – but it is essential to keep your nervous system running smoothly and, if you don't get it, your body can suffer irreversible damage. Vitamin B_{12} is found only in animal foods (including dairy and eggs); there are no plant sources. If you are a lacto-ovo vegetarian, you're covered. But if you are a vegan, or if you eat dairy and eggs only rarely, you need to make sure you get your daily dose. Some cereals, breads, pastas, crackers, non-dairy beverages (such as soy milk and rice milk), and meat substitutes (such as veggie burgers and tofu hot dogs) are fortified with B_{12}, so check the labels. One brand of nutritional yeast, Red Star Vegetarian Support Formula, contains vitamin B_{12}. If you aren't sure you're getting B_{12} in your food, take a supple-

ment. A store-brand multi-vitamin may be the most economical source of vitamin B_{12}.

Vitamin C

If you eat lots of fruits and vegetables, you probably get enough of this vitamin. It's especially abundant in cranberries, citrus fruits, tomatoes, strawberries, red and green peppers, dark green vegetables, and potatoes with skins. Vitamin C is essential to maintain healthy teeth, gums, and blood vessels.

Vitamin D

Vitamin D helps your body use calcium to keep your bones and teeth strong. It's found in fortified milk, margarine, and cereals. You also get vitamin D from sun exposure. So GO – get outside!

Minerals

Your body needs several different minerals to stay healthy. These three are the most critical for vegetarians.

Calcium

You need calcium to build strong bones. And not just during your growing years, but also as "insurance" against osteoporosis – weakened brittle bones caused by calcium loss, which can occur later in life. Kids between the ages of 11 and 19 should get 1200 milligrams of calcium a day. You'll find it in dairy products, seeds and nuts, legumes, figs, and blackstrap molasses. Dark green vegetables, especially kale and broccoli, are excellent sources, but spinach, Swiss chard, and beet greens are not, because they contain a substance that makes it hard to absorb the calcium. Some brands of orange juice and non-dairy milk (soy and rice) are fortified with calcium. As well, tofu that has been set with calcium salts (added to make the soy milk form curds) is a good source.

Iron

Iron makes up hemoglobin, the part of the blood that carries oxygen through your body, so it's important for healthy blood and circulation. Because they lose iron each month during menstruation, girls need more iron than boys do. The recommended intake for girls between the ages of 11 and 24 is 15 milligrams a day; for boys, it's 12 milligrams a day. Meat contains iron, but so do many plant foods, so you can get enough if you eat a varied diet. Foods that are high in iron include legumes (especially lentils, kidney beans, chick peas, and pinto beans), dark green vegetables, blackstrap molasses, dried fruits (such as dried apricots and raisins), tempeh, and some brands of tofu. Some breakfast cereals and meat substitutes are fortified with iron.

Iron + Vitamin C = Iron Boost

Want a couple of neat tricks to help your body absorb more iron? One is to cook food in cast-iron pans. Another is to eat iron-rich foods along with foods that are high in vitamin C. And that's a cinch, because there are plenty of combinations that naturally go together – like vegetarian chili with tomato sauce, or a stir-fry made with broccoli and red peppers, or a fruit salad sprinkled with raisins.

Zinc

This mineral helps you grow normally, develop sexually, heal wounds, taste, and smell. It's found in legumes, tofu, nuts and seeds, fortified meat substitutes (such as veggie burgers and tofu hot dogs), eggs, brewer's yeast, fortified cereals, whole wheat bread, and milk.

Food Groups for Vegetarians

Whole grains are high in carbohydrates, tofu is loaded with protein, almonds provide calcium, beans are full of iron.... Hold on! How are you supposed to remember which foods have which nutrients? And how on earth do you put it all together in a sane eating plan?

Relax. There's an easy way. Foods with similar nutrients are grouped into "families" called food groups. If you eat the right number of servings from all the food groups every day, you'll get a varied and healthy diet, with all the nutrients you need.

For vegetarians, the food groups are Grain Products; Vegetables and Fruits; Legumes, Eggs, Nuts, and Seeds; and Milk and Alternates. For each food group, the recommended number of servings for kids aged 10 to 17 is shown below. If you're growing, very active or underweight, try to eat the higher number of servings in the recommended range.

Grain Products

This group includes breads, cereals, pastas, grains, pancakes, and crackers. These foods provide carbohydrates, fiber, protein, B vitamins, and minerals. Eat 6 to 11 servings of grain products a day, and remember that whole grains are best.

Grain Products: What's a Serving?

1 slice of bread
1 roll or tortilla
½ bagel, pita bread, hamburger or hot dog bun
½ cup (125 mL) cooked cereal
¾ cup (175 mL) cold cereal
½ cup (125 mL) cooked pasta (any kind), rice, or other grain
1 small pancake, waffle, or muffin
2–6 crackers

Vegetables and Fruits

This group includes everything you can think of from garden, tree, or vine – fresh, frozen, cooked, juiced, or dried. Vegetables and fruits provide vitamins C and A, folic acid, calcium, and iron. Eat 5 to 10 servings a day.

Vegetables and Fruits: What's a Serving?

1 whole medium apple, orange, peach, banana, potato, or carrot
2 whole small fruits, such as apricots, plums, or mandarin oranges
½ cup (125 mL) very small fruits, such as cherries, grapes, or berries
½ cup (125 mL) canned or frozen fruit
1 cup (250 mL) raw vegetables or salad

½ cup (125 mL) cooked vegetables
½ cup (125 mL) juice
¼ cup (50 mL) dried fruit

Legumes, Eggs, Nuts, and Seeds

This group includes cooked beans and peas, tofu and other soy products, nuts and seeds and their butters, and eggs. These foods provide many of the same nutrients as meat: protein, iron, calcium, zinc, vitamin B$_6$, and fiber. Eat 2 to 4 servings a day from this group.

Legumes, Eggs, Nuts, and Seeds: What's a Serving?

½ cup (125 mL) tofu or tempeh

1 tofu burger or tofu hot dog

½ cup (125 mL) cooked beans (any kind), TVP, lentils, or split peas

2 tablespoons (25 mL) nuts, seeds, or nut or seed butter, such as peanut butter, tahini (sesame butter), or almond butter

1 egg

Milk and Alternates

This is the milk, cheese, and yogurt group, broadened to included non-dairy products that also provide calcium, zinc, protein, and vitamins D and B$_{12}$. Eat 3 servings of milk and alternates a day.

Milk and Alternates: What's a Serving?

1 cup (250 mL) fortified dairy or non-dairy (soy, rice, nut, etc.) milk

1-½ oz (42 g) dairy or soy cheese

¾ cup (175 mL) dairy or soy yogurt

Beyond the Food Groups

◆ Keep your body lubricated by drinking 6 to 8 glasses of water (or juice or herbal tea) every day.

◆ Vegans should include a source of vitamin B$_{12}$ in their diets along with a source of vitamin D if sun exposure is limited.

◆ Include 1 to 2 servings of healthy fats in your diet daily. Healthy fats come mainly from nuts, seeds, olives, and their oils. Good sources are walnuts, flaxseeds and flaxseed oil, hempseeds and hempseed oil, canola oil, olives and olive oil. One serving is 1 tablespoon (15 mL).

◆ You may have noticed that sugar, jam, honey, and syrup are not included in the food groups. Nor are seasonings such as mustard, ketchup, and soy sauce. Nor are soft drinks, candy bars, and chips. These foods are called "other foods" and, although they are part of our diet, they provide little nutrition. It's not necessary to cut them out entirely – after all, food would be bland without seasonings, and everybody enjoys a sweet treat occasionally – but try to use them in moderation.

Menu Planning

Okay, now it's time to put all this theory into practice. Just how do you get all of the servings you need into your day? That's where menu planning comes in. The following sample menus are examples of how to slot the recommended number of servings from the food groups into the meals and snacks a normal person eats in a day. Following each menu is a tally that shows how it meets the daily requirements for each food group.

Remember, these are only samples, not lists of exactly what you should eat. Go back to the food groups and substitute different foods. Play with color and flavor and texture. After all, eating isn't just about keeping us alive, it's about having fun, too.

What the Symbols Mean

Grain Products

Vegetables and Fruits

Legumes, Eggs, Nuts, and Seeds

Milk and Alternates

Menu #1:
Lacto-ovo Vegetarian Diet

Breakfast

Orange juice (½ cup/125 mL) =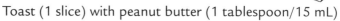

Bowl of cold whole-grain cereal (¾ cup/175 mL) with milk

(1 cup/250 mL) and banana (½ medium) = ✖ / 🥛 / ½ 🍅

Toast (1 slice) with peanut butter (1 tablespoon/15 mL)

= 🍅 / ½ 🥚

🌾

Snack

Apple (1) = 🍅

Rice cakes (2) with cheese (2 slices) = ✖ / ½ 🥚

🌾

Lunch

Egg salad sandwich (2 slices bread, 1 hard-boiled egg, 1 teaspoon/

5 mL low-fat mayonnaise) with lettuce (1 leaf) and tomato

(3 slices) = 2 ✖ / 🥚 / 🍅

Milk (1 cup/250 mL) = 🥛

Orange (1) = 🍅   Oatmeal raisin cookie (1)

🌾

Snack

Pear (1) = 🍅

Crackers (6) = ✖

Dinner

Vegetarian chili made with beans, tofu,
tomato sauce, and vegetables (1-½ cups/375 mL) = 2 /
Cornbread (1 large slice) with canola oil margarine = / (Fat)
Salad (1 cup/250 mL) with oil and vinegar dressing = /(Fat)
Fruit salad (1 cup/250 mL) = 2

Snack

Low-fat yogurt (¾ cup/175 mL) =
Graham crackers (4) =

Totals for Menu #1:		Recommended:
	9 servings	6–11 servings
	9-½ servings	5–10 servings
	4 servings	2–4 servings
	3 servings	3 servings
Fats	2 servings	1–2 servings

Menu #2:
Vegan Diet

Breakfast

Grapefruit juice (½ cup/125 mL) =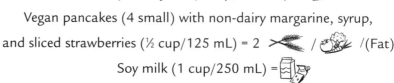

Vegan pancakes (4 small) with non-dairy margarine, syrup,

and sliced strawberries (½ cup/125 mL) = 2 ⟋ / 🥗 /(Fat)

Soy milk (1 cup/250 mL) = 🥛

Snack

Peach (1) = 🍅🥬

Handful of cashews = 🥜

Lunch

Pita sandwich with hummus (½ cup/125 mL),

shredded carrots, and lettuce = 2 ⟋ / 🥜 / 🥗

Soy milk (1 cup/250 mL) = 🥛

Apple (1) = 🍅🥬

Peanut butter square (1)

Snack

Bagel (1) with almond butter (2 tablespoons/25 mL)

= 2 ⟋ / 🥜

Dinner

Stir-fry with tofu (½ cup/125 mL), veggies (1 cup/250 mL),
and brown rice (1 cup/250 mL) = / 2 / 2

Salad (1 cup/250 mL) with oil and vinegar dressing = / (Fat)

Whole-grain roll (1) =

Melon (2 large slices) =

Snack

Fruit smoothie (½ banana, ½ cup/125 mL blueberries,
1 cup/250 mL soy milk) = 1-½ /

Muffin (1 large) = 2

Totals for Menu #2:

	Totals for Menu #2:	Recommended:
	11 servings	6–11 servings
	10-½ servings	5–10 servings
	4 servings	2–4 servings
	3 servings	3 servings
Fats	2 servings	1–2 servings

Try This

Now it's your turn. Divide a sheet of paper into sections labeled Breakfast, Snack, Lunch, etc., and make up a daily menu you'd like to eat. At the side, mark down the number of servings each food would provide from each food group, then add up your totals to make sure they match the recommended amounts. If necessary, adjust your menu to make it more nutritionally balanced.

Round-the-Clock Meal Ideas

With so many delicious grains, legumes, vegetables, fruits, nuts, and seeds to choose from, and so many different ways they can be combined, the creative possibilities of a vegetarian diet are nearly endless. But endless is a big word. The choices may seem daunting until you've had a chance to experiment and find your favorites. Here are suggestions for vegetarian meals to take you through the day. You'll find recipes for the starred dishes in the next chapter.

Breakfast

Most breakfast foods are already vegetarian (not counting bacon and sausage, of course!), so breakfast is the meal that changes the least when you become a vegetarian. Some tips:

◆ Try to eat from at least three of the four food groups at breakfast. A glass of juice and a bowl of cereal with milk will do it.

◆ Make whole grains the center of your morning meal. And think beyond oatmeal – there's also rice, quinoa, and millet.

◆ If you're a lacto-ovo, don't overdo it with eggs, cheese, and high-fat milk.

Breakfast Ideas

Peanut Cereal*

Tofu Scramble*

Vegan Pancakes*

Muffins with tahini or almond butter

Whole-grain Pudding*

Fruit with yogurt (dairy or soy) and granola

Easy Eggless Baking

Just because you don't eat eggs doesn't mean you can't enjoy baked goods. Commercial egg replacer is available in some stores. Soft tofu, mashed banana, or applesauce can be substituted in some recipes. You can also make your own egg replacer using ground flaxseeds; check a vegan cookbook for recipes.

Lunch

Sure, peanut butter and jam is vegetarian, but live a little! If sandwiches are your thing, experiment with different breads, fillings, and seasonings. Get away from the sandwich routine with cold pasta or grain salads, soups, and rice or noodle dishes. (Hint: Lots of the dinner suggestions make yummy lunches, too!)

- Try to include foods from at least three of the four food groups.

- If you're eating cheese, choose lower-fat varieties.

- Choose lower-fat higher-nutrition seasonings and spreads (for example, mustard, ketchup, tahini, or almond butter) instead of mayonnaise or butter.

Lunch Sandwich Ideas

Where's-the-Egg Salad* in pita or a roll

Pita with Hummus* or falafel and shredded veggies and sprouts

Bean spread (mash and season your favorite beans) in a tortilla

Peanut (or almond or cashew) butter and banana on a bagel

Tofu deli slices on rye bread

Almond-Ricotta Spread* on whole-grain toast

Leftover nut or lentil loaf on a multi-grain roll (good with
ketchup or mustard)

Dinner

There are two approaches you can take to the evening meal.
You can keep your dinner plate as it was before, replacing the
meat with a vegetarian substitute such as eggs, a tofu patty or
hot dog, tempeh, or beans. Or you can get creative with dishes
based on grains, legumes, vegetables, and dairy products.
Either way, dinner can be a delicious and satisfying meal.

◆ Try to have at least three of the four food groups in your
dinner meal, including at least one serving from the
Legumes, Eggs, Nuts, and Seeds group.

◆ When you're cooking grains, beans, or pasta, make extra
and keep it in the fridge or freezer. Then you can whip up
a quick meal by throwing on tomato or other sauce, tofu,
nuts, vegetables, or cheese.

◆ If your family is having pasta for dinner, save some sauce
before the meat goes in. Make yourself a rich healthy sauce
by stirring in tofu, vegetables, beans, or nuts.

◆ Turn a salad into a meal by adding cheese, nuts, tofu, or
beans (chick peas add crunch and a nutty flavor). Or try a
grain-based salad using rice, millet, bulgur, or quinoa, with
the same toppings.

- Think of soup not as a first course but as dinner. Hearty bean, lentil, or split-pea soups – with whole-grain rolls, slices of dairy or soy cheese, and a side salad – make a filling and nutritious meal, especially on cold winter nights.

- Cheat a little. Just because you're a vegetarian doesn't mean you have to slave in the kitchen. Keep convenience foods on hand: canned beans, prepared pizza and pie crusts, baking mixes, grated cheese, frozen veggie or tofu burgers. See below for a complete list of vegetarian foods to stock up on.

Dinner Ideas

Vegetable Pancakes* (the veggies can be incorporated into the cakes or rolled up inside)

Vegetarian Chili*

Burritos or enchiladas

Vegetarian lasagna

Spaghetti and Nut Balls*

Pizza

Tofu or Vegetable Pot Pie*

Stir-fry of veggies and tofu over pasta or grains

Lentil loaf

Nut loaf or patties

Hearty Bean or Vegetable Soup*

Wraps filled with grains, beans, vegetables, and sauce

Snacks

Recess, after school, before bed... snacks are great anytime, and they fit into a vegetarian diet as easily as you can say "popcorn." If you're growing, very active, or underweight, snacks are a good way to boost your energy and your nutrient intake throughout the day.

- ◆ As much as possible, choose snacks from the food groups. And during the day, eat snacks from different groups – for example, crackers at recess, trail mix after school, fruit in the evening.
- ◆ Once in a while is okay, but generally stay away from snacks that are high in fat, sugar, and salt.

Snack Ideas

Yogurt (soy or dairy)
Fruit, fresh, dried or in "leather" form (try fruit kabobs with a yogurt dip)
Popcorn
Crackers with cheese or nut butter
Raw veggies with a yogurt or Hummus* dip
Celery or apple slices spread with peanut butter
Fruit Smoothies* made with tofu (soft or silken) or milk (dairy or soy)
Frozen fruit juice popsicles
English muffin pizzas
Muffins, Scones*, or cookies, preferably whole-grain and low-fat
Trail mix
Grain or "power" bars

Food Frontiers
Think Grill

Going to a barbecue? Even if hamburgers and hot dogs are on the grill, you don't have to go hungry. Plenty of vegetarian foods are great grilled. Here are some suggestions:

- ◆ Firm tofu, thickly sliced and marinated in the sauce of your choice

- Grilled veggies – zucchini, eggplant, yellow, red or green peppers, onions, and mushrooms – brushed lightly with olive oil and sprinkled with herbs
- Tofu-and-veggie kabobs
- Tofu hot dogs and veggie burgers
- Corn on the cob

Liv, 17: We were at a barbecue at the home of friends of my parents', and their son was going on about how he loved hamburgers and hated vegetarian food. I had brought my own tofu burgers to grill. I gave him one in a bun with all the toppings but I didn't tell him what it was. He wolfed it down and said, "That was the best burger I've ever eaten!" Then I told him he'd just eaten a tofu burger. Boy, was he mad!

Around the World

Think ethnic – and open up your world. There are dozens of ethnic cuisines to choose from, and many feature vegetarian foods. When you're eating out, ethnic restaurants often have more vegetarian choices than standard restaurants. Even if some dishes traditionally include meat, you can request a vegetarian version. Some great international dishes:

- Middle Eastern: falafel and hummus in pita, eggplant dishes, lentil dishes
- Italian: pasta, risotto, pizza, veggie calzone
- Indian: curries, dal, vegetable samosas, chick pea dishes, vegetable combos
- Mexican: burritos, enchiladas, tostadas – anything with beans, rice, and tortillas
- Thai: pad Thai, hot and sour soup
- Chinese: chop suey, tofu dishes, chow mein, vegetables in black bean sauce

Vegetarian Foods to Stock Up On

It's a good idea to keep a variety of vegetarian foods on hand. That way, you can whip up meals quickly and easily. Often, foods are cheaper when bought in bulk. But beware of buying too much at a time – if unused, the food will go stale. Here are some suggestions for having a well-stocked kitchen, beyond the usual staples that most households have. (R means keep refrigerated, and F means frozen.)

Grain Products

Brown rice
Packaged, seasoned rice mixes
Other grains: millet, couscous, quinoa, kasha
Wheat germ (R)
Whole grain cereals, hot and cold
Pastas
Whole-grain flours (wheat, soy, cornmeal, buckwheat)

Vegetables and Fruits

Canned tomatoes, tomato sauce, and tomato paste
Canned or frozen fruit
Mixed vegetables for stir-frying (F)
Dried fruit

Legumes

Dried legumes (lentils, split peas, chick peas, kidney beans, pinto beans)
Canned legumes
Tofu (R)
Tempeh (R or F)
Soy or tofu deli slices, hot dogs, patties (R or F)
Veggie patties (R or F)
Instant mixes (for falafel, soups, etc.)

Nuts and Seeds

Nuts (almonds, pecans, cashews, peanuts, walnuts) (R or F)

Seeds (sesame, sunflower, pumpkin) (R or F)

Nut and seed butters (peanut, almond, tahini) (R)

Other Foods

Nutritional yeast (preferably Red Star Vegetarian Support Formula)

Miso (R)

Vegetable broth powder or cubes

Soy sauce or tamari

Beano™

Where to Find Vegetarian Foods

◆ Grocery stores: Check bulk sections or ethnic or natural foods aisles.

◆ Natural or health-food stores: Many carry everything from frozen veggie dinners to animal-friendly cosmetics.

◆ Ethnic groceries: Check out Chinese, Japanese, Indian, Middle Eastern, Mexican, Greek, and African food shops.

◆ Farmers' markets: The place to go for fresh, often organic, produce in season.

◆ Food Co-ops: Because of bulk buying, prices are usually lower than at regular stores.

◆ Mail Order Companies: Some companies distribute natural foods by mail. Check ads in vegetarian magazines (see a list of magazines in the "Off You Go!" section), or contact your provincial, state, or national health-food association to get the names of companies.

Let's Get Cooking!

You've got the basics of nutrition and meal planning. You're prepared to handle people's reactions. Now it's time for the fun part of the book – eating! This chapter takes you into the kitchen with delicious vegetarian recipes.

Basic cooking instructions and safety tips are not included here – but they are important. If you do not know how to prepare a certain food or how to work safely in the kitchen, make sure you ask an adult or consult a basic cookbook.

The recipes are organized according to breakfast, lunch, dinner, and so on. But don't feel bound by traditional categories. Tofu Scramble works equally well as a dinner dish as it does a breakfast dish, and who says you can't eat Vegetarian Chili for a midnight snack? Feel free to mix up the recipes and try them any time of the day.

The recipes are labeled Lacto-ovo Vegetarian, Lacto Vegetarian, Vegan, etc. In many cases, by making a few substitutions, you

can easily turn a Vegetarian dish into a Vegan one. Look for the Veganize It! option at the end of the recipe.

Remember, these recipes are only a sampling; there are dozens of excellent sources of vegetarian and vegan recipes, so check out the cookbooks, magazines, and websites in the next chapter.

Now... let's get cooking. *Bon appétit!*

Beverages

Fruity Smoothie

Lacto Vegetarian

A breakfast pick-me-up or refreshing snack. Makes two servings.

1 banana
1 cup (250 mL) fresh, frozen or canned fruit (berries, cherries, peaches, apricots, mango, or pineapple)
1 tablespoon (15 mL) honey
1-½ cups (375 mL) milk

Put all ingredients into a blender and blend until creamy. For a frothier shake, crush 4 to 6 ice cubes in the blender before adding the other ingredients.

Veganize It!

Substitute brown sugar or maple syrup for the honey, and soy or rice milk for the dairy milk.

Yogurt Shake

Lacto Vegetarian

A thick shake with a refreshing tang. Makes one serving.

¾ cup (175 mL) vanilla-flavored yogurt

2 tablespoons (25 mL) skim milk powder

½ cup (125 mL) orange or pineapple juice

2 tablespoons (25 mL) honey

Combine all ingredients in a blender and blend until smooth.

Veganize It!

Substitute soy yogurt for the dairy yogurt, brown sugar for the honey, and soft silken tofu for the milk powder.

Breakfast

Peanut Cereal

Lacto Vegetarian

If you like the taste of peanut butter, you'll love this nourishing hot cereal. Makes two servings.

2 cups (500 mL) milk

½ cup (125 mL) whole-wheat flour

½ cup (125 mL) peanut meal (Grind roasted or raw peanuts in a
   blender or food processor until they form a meal.)

¼ cup (50 mL) raisins

1–2 tablespoons (15–25 mL) honey, to taste

Heat the milk in a saucepan over medium heat. Add the flour and peanut meal, using a wire whisk to stir the mixture smooth. When it comes to a boil, turn down heat to medium-low and cook uncovered for about 10 minutes or until the mixture thickens, stirring occasionally. Stir in the raisins and honey.

Veganize It!

Use soy milk instead of dairy milk, and brown sugar instead of honey.

What does one legume say to another legume when it's time to leave?

Let's split, pea.

91

Vegan Pancakes

Vegan

Makes two to four servings.

1 cup (250 mL) flour (whole-wheat or a mixture of whole-wheat and unbleached white)
1 tablespoon (15 mL) baking powder
1 cup (250 mL) soy or rice milk
2 tablespoons (25 mL) vegetable oil

Combine the dry ingredients in one bowl and the wet ingredients in another. Add the wet ingredients to the dry and mix just until moistened; don't overbeat. Heat a frying pan or griddle over medium-high heat and spray with non-stick spray or add a little vegetable oil. When a drop of water sizzles in the pan, it's ready. Pour in about ½ cup (125 mL) of batter for each pancake. Cook the cakes until small bubbles appear on the top, then flip and cook on the other side. Serve with toppings of your choice.

Variations

Oatmeal Pancakes: For a crunchy texture, add ¼ cup (50 mL) rolled oats and a dash of cinnamon to the batter.
Fruit Pancakes: Add a handful of fresh or frozen blueberries to the batter. Or serve berries or sliced peaches or bananas on top.
Decadent Dessert Pancakes: Add 2 tablespoons (25 mL) sweetener (brown sugar, maple syrup, or rice syrup) along with ¼ cup (50 mL) non-dairy chocolate chips. Drizzle chocolate syrup on top.

How do Japanese vegetarians procrastinate?

They do it tamari.

92

Tofu Scramble

Vegan

A yummy substitute for scrambled eggs and a great brunch dish. Makes two to four servings.

16 oz (500 g) firm tofu

2 tablespoons (25 mL) vegetable oil

1-½ cups (375 mL) chopped mixed vegetables (any combination of onions, mushrooms, green, red or yellow peppers, zucchini, broccoli, etc.)

1 clove garlic, peeled and finely chopped

2 teaspoons (10 mL) tamari or regular soy sauce

1 tablespoon (15 mL) nutritional yeast, preferably Red Star Vegetarian Support Formula (optional)

seasonings to taste: parsley, oregano, cumin, turmeric, black pepper, or chili powder

Before cooking, drain excess water from the tofu: place it on a plate, put another plate on top, add a weight such as a large can of tomatoes, let it sit for 10–15 minutes, and drain off the water. Mash the tofu with a fork.

Heat the oil in a skillet and sauté the vegetables for 5 minutes, stirring frequently. Add the garlic and tofu and sauté for another 5 minutes, stirring frequently. Add the soy sauce, nutritional yeast, and seasonings and cook for 1 more minute. For a hearty brunch, serve with home-fried potatoes and whole-grain toast.

Variation

Mexican Scramble: Season with cumin and chili powder, and serve in warm tortillas with salsa on top. *Olé!*

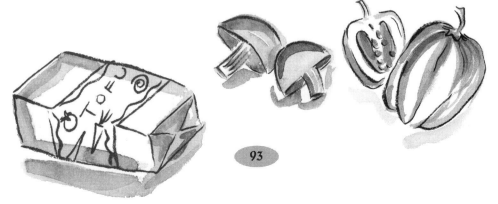

Whole-grain Pudding

Lacto Vegetarian

A quick yet satisfying breakfast – and a great way to use up leftover grains. Makes one serving.

1 cup (250 mL) cooked rice, quinoa, millet, or other grain
½ cup (125 mL) milk
2 tablespoons (25 mL) honey
2 tablespoons (25 mL) raisins
dash each of cinnamon and nutmeg

Combine all ingredients in a microwave-safe container and heat until milk bubbles. To cook in the oven, combine ingredients in a small baking dish and bake at 350°F for 10–15 minutes. For variety, add chopped apples, blueberries, sliced bananas, or a sprinkle of walnuts or pecans.

Veganize It!
Replace the dairy milk with soy or rice milk, and use brown sugar or maple syrup instead of honey.

Soups

Potato-Cheese Soup

Lacto Vegetarian

Makes four servings.

2 large potatoes, peeled and diced

1 tablespoon (15 mL) oil

1 medium onion, chopped

1 clove of garlic, chopped

1 cup (250 mL) greens (spinach, kale, beet greens, etc.), chopped

2 tablespoons (25 mL) margarine or butter

¼ cup (50 mL) flour

1 cup (250 mL) milk

1 cup (250 mL) grated cheese (low-fat Cheddar, Edam,
  Monterey Jack, Gouda, etc.)

salt and pepper to taste

½ teaspoon (2.5 mL) each dried parsley, thyme, and savory

Put potatoes in a soup pot and add water to cover. Cover pot, bring to a boil, and simmer for 10–15 minutes, until potatoes are medium-soft. Remove about half of the potatoes, mash them, and return them to the pot. In a pan, sauté onion in 1 tablespoon (15 mL) oil for about 5 minutes. Add garlic and greens and sauté for another minute. Add to potatoes along with salt, pepper, and herbs. In a saucepan, melt margarine or butter, add flour, and stir with a wire whisk until the flour is lightly browned. Add milk a little at a time, whisking after each addition to smooth out lumps. When all the milk has been added, stir over low heat until the mixture thickens. Turn off heat and stir in cheese. Five minutes before serving, stir the cheese sauce into the potatoes. Add water if the soup is too thick. Adjust seasonings to taste and reheat.

Veganize It!

Use oil instead of butter or margarine, soy milk in place of dairy milk, and soy cheese instead of dairy cheese.

Chick Pea-Nut Soup

Vegan

Mellow chick pea flavor – with a twist. Makes four servings.

1 cup (250 mL) dry chick peas and 3 cups (750 mL) water
  OR two 14 oz (398 mL) cans of chick peas
1 tablespoon (15 mL) oil
1 small onion, chopped
2 medium carrots, sliced
1 vegetable stock cube or 1 tablespoon (15 mL) vegetable broth powder
2 tablespoons (25 mL) peanut butter
1 teaspoon (5 mL) cumin
1 teaspoon (5 mL) fresh or dried parsley

If using dry chick peas, pick over and discard any pebbles or discolored beans. Rinse. Bring water to a boil, add chick peas and simmer for 1-½ hours. If using canned chick peas, empty cans into a soup pot. You should have 2-3 cups of cooked chick peas. Remove ½ cup (125 mL) of chick peas from the pot and reserve.

Sauté onions and carrots in oil for about 5 minutes. Add to chick peas along with remaining ingredients. Stir until vegetable broth cube or powder dissolves. Place soup ingredients in a blender or food processor and purée until smooth. (You may have to do this in batches to avoid overflowing or clogging the blender, and you may have to add more water if the mixture is too thick.) Return to soup pot and add the reserved chick peas. Add salt and pepper to taste. Reheat.

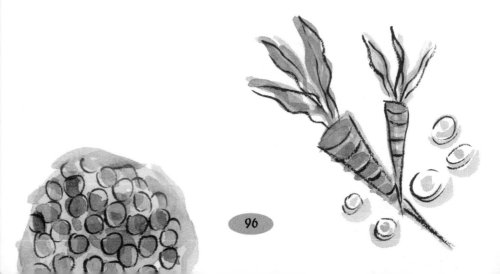

Sandwich Fillings

Where's-the-Egg Salad

Vegan

Makes two to four servings.

8 oz (250 g) medium or firm tofu

1 tablespoon (15 mL) tofunaise (a mayonnaise substitute)

1 stalk celery, chopped fine

1 green onion, chopped fine

½ teaspoon (2.5 mL) mustard

fresh or dried parsley and dill

salt and pepper to taste

Drain tofu and mash with a fork. Add the remaining ingredients and mix thoroughly. Serve between slices of bread or in pitas with sprouts and lettuce, or scoop up with crackers.

Variations

Add a sprinkle of curry powder or a dash of hot sauce.
For crunch, add roasted sunflower seeds.
To boost nutrition, add 1 teaspoon (5 mL) nutritional yeast, preferably Red Star Vegetarian Support Formula.

Almond-Ricotta Spread

Lacto Vegetarian

A slightly sweet spread that's good on toast or crackers. Makes four servings.

1 cup (250 mL) almond butter

1 cup (250 mL) low-fat ricotta cheese

1 tablespoon (15 mL) honey

Mix all ingredients together. That's it!

Hummus

Vegan

The Middle Eastern favorite – great for parties. Makes four to six servings.

one 19 oz (540 mL) can of chick peas, drained
  OR 2 cups (500 mL) cooked chick peas
¼ cup (50 mL) tahini (sesame paste)
¼ cup (50 mL) lemon juice (bottled or fresh)
1 or 2 cloves of garlic, minced
2 tablespoons (25 mL) fresh parsley, chopped fine
salt and pepper to taste

Put all ingredients in a food processor and purée until smooth.
Or mash the chick peas by hand and mix in the other ingredients.
Serve with pita bread, bagel chips, or crackers.

Dinner

Veggie Pancakes

Lacto-ovo Vegetarian

Who says pancakes are only for breakfast? These delicious cakes make a satisfying evening meal. Makes four servings.

3 cups (750 mL) chopped vegetables (any combination of carrots, onions, peas, corn, zucchini, mushrooms, broccoli, etc.)

2 tablespoons (25 mL) oil

2 cups (500 mL) flour (whole-wheat or a mixture of whole-wheat and unbleached white)

¼ cup (50 mL) wheat germ

1 tablespoon (15 mL) nutritional yeast, preferably Red Star Vegetarian Support Formula

1 tablespoon (15 mL) baking powder

1 egg

2 tablespoons (25 mL) oil

1 cup (250 mL) milk

salt and pepper to taste

a sprinkle each of parsley, basil, and oregano, or any combination of herbs

Sauté the vegetables in 2 tablespoons (25 mL) oil for 5–10 minutes, or until tender. In a large mixing bowl, stir together the flour, wheat germ, nutritional yeast, baking powder, salt, pepper, and herbs. In a separate bowl, beat together the egg, 2 tablespoons (25 mL) oil, and milk. Add to the dry ingredients and mix. Stir in the vegetables. Heat a large frying pan and spray with non-stick spray or add a few drops of oil. When the pan is hot, pour on about ¾ cup (175 mL) of batter for each pancake. Cook until bubbles form on top, then flip and cook on the other side. As the pancakes are done, keep them warm in a baking pan in the oven on low heat. Serve with grated cheese, applesauce, or sour cream – or all three!

Veganize It!

Replace the egg with an equivalent amount of egg replacer, and use soy milk instead of dairy milk. For toppings, use grated soy cheese and soy sour cream.

Vegetarian Chili

Vegan

Rib-sticking chili – as hot as you like it! Makes six servings.

1 cup (250 mL) dry beans (kidney, pinto, black, navy, etc.)
   and 3 cups (750 mL) water OR two 14 oz (398 mL) cans of drained
   beans, for a total of about 3 cups (750 mL) cooked beans

¼ cup (50 mL) dry TVP

½ cup (125 mL) firm tofu, chopped

one 14 oz (398 mL) can of whole or diced tomatoes

¼ cup (50 mL) tomato paste

1 tablespoon (15 mL) blackstrap molasses

1 medium onion, chopped

2 medium carrots, chopped

2 stalks of celery, chopped

½ cup (125 mL) frozen or canned corn

1 or 2 jalapeño peppers, fresh or bottled (optional)

1 tablespoon (15 mL) soy sauce

1 teaspoon (5 mL) cumin

1 tablespoon fresh cilantro, chopped

black pepper or chili powder to taste

In a large oven-proof pot, cook the beans in the water for 1 hour.
Turn off the heat, add the TVP, cover and let sit for 5 minutes or until
the TVP is reconstituted. (If using canned beans, drain, cover with
fresh water, bring to a boil, turn off the heat, add TVP, and let sit.)
Preheat oven to 325°F. Add the remaining ingredients to the beans.
If the tomatoes are whole, cut into chunks. Cover pot and bake for
1–2 hours, stirring occasionally. Remove the jalapeño peppers and
discard. Return pot to oven, uncovered, and bake for another ½ hour
to 1 hour. Serve with warm cornbread.

Variation

Enchiladas: Bake the chili uncovered for a longer period of time so
that more of the liquid evaporates. Put a large spoonful of chili in a
corn or wheat tortilla, sprinkle with grated Cheddar or Jack cheese
(dairy or soy), roll up, and reheat in the oven until the cheese melts.

Tofu-Veggie Pot Pie
Vegan

Makes four to six servings.

one double pie crust (store-bought or home-made)

2 tablespoons (25 mL) oil

8 oz (250 g) firm tofu, cubed

2 cups (500 mL) vegetables (any combination of onions, mushrooms, carrots, zucchini, peas, green beans, turnips, kale, Swiss chard, etc.), chopped

1 potato, cooked and diced

2 tablespoons oil

¼ cup (50 mL) flour

2 tablespoons (25 mL) nutritional yeast, preferably Red Star Vegetarian Support Formula

1-½ cups (375 mL) liquid (soy milk, vegetable broth, or a combination)

1 teaspoon (5 mL) each of parsley, thyme, and sage

salt and pepper to taste

If making your own pie crust, follow any standard recipe, using non-dairy margarine in place of regular margarine or butter, and whole-wheat pastry flour or a mixture of whole-wheat and unbleached white flours. If using store-bought crust, thaw it if it is frozen. Put the bottom crust in an oiled pie plate.

Heat 2 tablespoons (25 mL) oil in a large skillet and sauté vegetables for 5–10 minutes, until crisp-tender. Add the tofu and sauté for another 5 minutes. Stir in the potato. In a saucepan, heat the oil, add the flour, and stir with a wire whisk until the flour is lightly browned. Add the liquid a little at a time, whisking after each addition to smooth out lumps. When all the liquid has been added, stir over low heat until the mixture thickens. Turn off heat and stir in the nutritional yeast, herbs, and seasonings. Preheat oven to 350°F. Put the vegetable and tofu mixture in the pie shell. Pour on the sauce, poking the vegetables gently to make sure they are covered. Put on the top crust, press the edges of the two crusts together to seal, and prick the top crust in several places with a fork to allow steam to escape. Bake for 30–40 minutes or until the top crust is golden brown.

Spaghetti and Nut Balls

Lacto Vegetarian

Your meat-eating friends may say these are the best "meatballs" they've ever tasted! Makes four to six servings.

1-¼ cups (300 mL) nuts and seeds (a good combination is
  ½ cup/125 mL walnuts, ½ cup/125 mL pecans or almonds,
  and ¼ cup/50 mL sunflower or pumpkin seeds)
  (Note: You may use raw or roasted nuts, but roasted will give a
  richer flavor.)
1 cup (250 mL) rolled oats
½ cup (125 mL) medium tofu
salt and pepper to taste
vegetable oil as needed
8 oz (250 g) spaghetti (try whole-wheat, spinach-flavored, or
  herbed varieties)
2 cups (500 mL) store-bought or home-made pasta sauce
grated Parmesan cheese, optional

Put nuts and seeds in a food processor and grind to a coarse meal. Add oats and grind until the mixture has an even fine consistency. Add tofu, salt, and pepper and process briefly until the mixture is thick and moistened. (Depending on how wet your tofu is, you may need to add a little more.) With your fingers, form mixture into walnut-sized balls; it will be sticky. Heat a little oil in a saucepan. Fry nut balls several a time on both sides until golden brown. Watch carefully; add oil as needed and turn the nut balls frequently to prevent burning. Place them on paper towels to drain excess oil.

Make home-made pasta sauce, or heat up bottled sauce in a saucepan or microwave-safe container. Cook spaghetti in plenty of boiling water for 10 minutes or according to package instructions. Drain in a colander. For each serving, put spaghetti on a plate, top with 3 or 4 nut balls, spoon on sauce, and sprinkle with cheese, if desired.

Veganize It!

Top with grated soy cheese instead of Parmesan cheese.

Baked Goods and Desserts

Cornbread

Lacto-ovo Vegetarian

The perfect accompaniment to chili, soup, or stew. Makes six servings.

1 cup (250 mL) cornmeal
1 cup (250 mL) flour
1 tablespoon (15 mL) baking powder
¼ cup (50 mL) sugar
1 egg
1 cup (250 mL) milk
¼ cup (50 mL) oil

Preheat oven to 350°F. In a large mixing bowl, mix dry ingredients together. Make a "well" or dent in the middle of the dry ingredients, add the wet ingredients, and mix until well blended. Pour into an oiled 9-inch square baking pan. Bake for 20–25 minutes.

Veganize It!

Omit the egg. Add ½ teaspoon (2.5 mL) baking soda to the dry ingredients. Replace the dairy milk with 1-¼ cups (300 mL) soy milk or rice milk plus 1 teaspoon (5 mL) vinegar. Mix as above.

Peanut Butter Balls

Vegetarian

These high-energy treats are great for hiking – and for your sweet tooth. Makes about 12 balls.

1 cup (250 mL) peanut butter
½ cup (125 mL) honey
1 cup (250 mL) granola
½ cup (125 mL) sunflower seeds or sesame seeds
½ teaspoon (2.5 mL) vanilla
wheat germ or coconut

Mix first five ingredients together. Form into walnut-sized balls and roll in wheat germ or coconut.

Veganize It!

Substitute brown sugar or maple syrup for the honey.

Oatmeal Scones

Lacto Vegetarian

Traditionally, scones contain eggs and cream so, technically speaking, these aren't scones. But they're just as delicious, especially warm right out of the oven! Makes eight to ten scones.

1 cup (250 mL) rolled oats
1-¼ cups (300 mL) whole-wheat pastry flour (or a mixture of whole-wheat and unbleached white flours)
¼ cup (50 mL) wheat germ
½ cup (125 mL) granola
½ cup (125 mL) brown sugar
1 tablespoon (15 mL) baking powder
1 teaspoon (5 mL) baking soda
¼ cup (50 mL) oil
½ cup (125 mL) buttermilk

Preheat oven to 350°F. In a large mixing bowl, mix dry ingredients together. Make a "well" or dent in the middle of the dry ingredients and add the oil and buttermilk. Stir with just a few strokes until the dry ingredients are moistened; don't overmix. (You may need a little more liquid.) Place mounds of about ½ cup (125 mL) of dough on an oiled baking sheet. Bake for about 15 minutes.

Veganize It!

In place of buttermilk, use soy milk with 1 teaspoon (5 mL) vinegar added.

Variations

Add any of the following: chopped apples, blueberries, blackberries, raisins, dates, prunes, chopped walnuts or pecans, cinnamon, nutmeg, orange or lemon zest.

Chocolate Cake
Vegan

Who says vegans can't enjoy rich, decadent chocolate cake? Makes a two-layer cake.

3 cups (750 mL) whole-wheat pastry flour or unbleached white flour
2 teaspoons (10 mL) baking soda
¾ cup (375 mL) cocoa powder
¾ cup (375 mL) non-dairy margarine
2 cups (500 mL) brown sugar
¼ cup (50 mL) water
2 cups (500 mL) soy milk
2 teaspoons (10 mL) vanilla

Preheat oven to 350°F. Sift cocoa, flour, and baking soda into a mixing bowl. Stir vanilla into milk. In a separate bowl, cream margarine and brown sugar. Add water gradually and beat well. Add the flour to the margarine mixture, alternating with the milk. Beat until smooth. Pour into two oiled 9-inch baking pans and bake for about 30 minutes.

Chocolate Icing
Vegan

2 cups (500 ml) icing sugar
⅓ cup (90 ml) cocoa powder
¼ cup (50 ml) non-dairy margarine
1 teaspoon (5 mL) vanilla
about ¼ cup (50 mL) soy milk

Sift together the cocoa and icing sugar. Add the margarine and vanilla and cream until smooth. Add the milk a little at a time, beating well after each addition, until the icing reaches spreading consistency.

Off You Go!

Organizations

EarthSave International
1509 Seabright Avenue, Suite B1
Santa Cruz, California, USA 95062
Web: www.earthsave.org
An international organization with national chapters. Promotes lifestyle choices that are healthy for both people and the planet. Publishes the *Healthy School Lunch Action Guide*. The website has vegetarian news, nutrition info, frequently asked questions (FAQs), a VegPledge, book listings, newsletters, and recipes.

International Vegetarian Union
In North America: PO Box 9710
Washington, DC, USA 20016
Web: www.ivu.org
Also includes Vegetarian Union of North America
Web: www.ivu.org/vuna
One of the longest-established vegetarian organizations, with national branches. The website has articles, a list of famous vegetarians by category, and vegetarian phrases in different languages. Youth Pages include games, articles by and about teens, book listings, and info about vegetarian musicians and bands.

North American Vegetarian Society
PO Box 72
Dolgeville, New York, USA 13329
Web: www.navs-online.org
Publishes *Vegetarian Voice* and *Vegetarian Voice Online!* Holds an annual Vegetarian Summerfest. The website has links to vegetarian organizations, lists of vegetarian restaurants, recipes, and info about sites for teens and kids.

People for the Ethical Treatment of Animals
501 Front Street
Norfolk, Virginia, USA 23510
Web: www.peta-online.org
The largest animal rights organization in the world. The website includes a kids' section with articles and *GRRR!*, an online magazine with news, contests, quizzes, and ways that kids can get involved.

Toronto Vegetarian Association

2300 Yonge Street, Suite 1101
Toronto, Ontario, Canada M4P 1E4
Web: www.veg.on.ca
Hosts community activities in greater Toronto, publishes a directory of vegetarian-friendly restaurants in Toronto and Canada, and provides fact sheets on nutrition, animal rights, and other vegetarian issues. The website has links to other organizations and resources, recipes, and a newsletter.

Vegetarian Resource Group

PO Box 1463
Baltimore, Maryland, USA 21203
Web: www.vrg.org
A very helpful organization that provides nutritional info for adults and children, recipes, and a list of cookbooks. Holds an annual essay contest for kids. The website includes a vegetarian page for kids, excerpts from Vegetarian Journal, travel info, a vegetarian quiz game, and tips on vegetarian food for camping and backpacking.

Vegetarian Youth Network

PO Box 1141
New Paltz, New York, USA 12561
Web: www.geocities.com
An organization run entirely by and for teenagers who support vegetarian and vegan living. Provides information about the advantages of going vegetarian or vegan, as well as recipes, vegetarian resources, and sources for products. The Vegetarian Youth Online website page provides links to other vegetarian kids and pen pals all over the world.

Youth for Environmental Sanity

420 Bronco Road
Soquel, California, USA 95073-9510
Web: www.yesworld.org
Founded by teens, YES puts an emphasis on social justice and environmental sanity. Holds camps, workshops, and events. The website has info about camps and other resources including books, guides, and articles.

Websites

About Veggie Cuisine
Web: http://vegsource.com
News, articles, books, and links to other vegetarian websites. Has a Veggie Youth section with questions and messages from vegetarian readers.

Famous Veggie
Web: www.famousveggie.com
Veggie cartoons, FAQs, nutritional information, lists of and quotes from famous vegetarians, news stories.

For New Vegetarians
Web: www.newveg.av.org
Lists products, books, profiles of famous vegetarians, and cartoons. Includes "How to Be a Vegetarian in 10 Easy Steps."

Vegan.com
Web: www.vegan.com
Book reviews, articles, FAQs, and more.

Vegetarian Dining
Web: www.vegdining.com
A guide to more than 2000 vegetarian restaurants around the world.

Veggie News
Web: www.veggienews.ca
A Canadian online vegetarian magazine. Has info about books, recipes, articles, a free vegetarian starter kit, and discussion page.

Magazines

Ahimsa
PO Box H
Malaga, New Jersey, USA 08328
Published by the American Vegan Society. Contains news and articles of interest to vegans, recipes, product information, etc.

Vegetarian Journal
Published by the Vegetarian Resource Group. See Organizations for the address.

Vegetarian Times
9 Riverbend Drive
Stamford, Connecticut, USA 06907
Web: www.vegetariantimes.com
Recipes and articles, book reviews, food and cooking information, and sources of natural-living products.

Vegetarian Voice
Published by the North American Vegetarian Society.
See Organizations for the address.

Veggie Life
1041 Shary Circle
Concord, California, USA 94518
Web: www.veggielife.com
Cooking tips and techniques, recipes, articles and advice on health, organic gardening, fitness, etc.

Books

Becoming Vegan. Summertown, Tennessee: Book Publishing Co., 2000; and **Becoming Vegetarian**. Toronto: Macmillan Canada, 1994. Both by Vesanto Melina, Brenda Davis, and Victoria Harrison. Extensive nutritional and health information, food groups, menus, and recipes.

Diet for a Small Planet by Frances Moore Lappé. New York: Ballantine Books, 1991. The "classic" that made the case for plant-based eating.

Food: Feasts, Cooks and Kitchens by Richard Tames. New York: Franklin Watts, 1994. Food history and trivia.

May All Be Fed: A Diet for a New World by John Robbins. New York: Morrow/Avon, 1993. An argument for a more just agriculture and food system.

Spill the Beans and Pass the Peanuts: Legumes by Meredith Sayles Hughes. Minneapolis: Lerner Publishing Co., 1999. History and science of different legumes.

A Teen's Guide to Going Vegetarian by Judy Krizmanic. New York: Puffin Books, 1994. Why teens become vegetarians, how to handle problem situations, nutritional info, vegetarian food groups, menus, recipes, and resources for more information.

Tomatoes, Potatoes, Corn, and Beans by Sylvia A. Johnson. New York: Atheneum, 1997. History and botany of important foods.

Vegetarian Handbook: A new guide to eating healthy across Canada by Toronto Vegetarian Association. Toronto: Toronto Vegetarian Association, 1996. Over 650 listings of vegetarian-friendly places from Newfoundland to Vancouver Island, including vacation spots, summer camps for kids, etc.

Vegetarian Journal's Guide to Natural Food Restaurants in the US and Canada by Vegetarian Resource Group. Garden City Park, NY: Avery Publishing Group, 1993. An indispensable travel companion.

Vegetarian Times Vegetarian Beginner's Guide by the editors of *Vegetarian Times* magazine. New York: Simon and Schuster Children's, 1996. Nutritional information, meal planning, recipes, and tips for getting started.

We're Talking About Vegetarianism by Samantha Calvert. East Sussex, England: Wayland, 1997. Why real-life kids became vegetarians, food groups and nutritional info, famous vegetarians, and great vegetarian foods.

Cookbooks

The Compassionate Cook by Ingrid Newkirk and People for the Ethical Treatment of Animals. New York: Warner Books, 1993. Vegan recipes with a conscience.

Foods From Mother Earth: A Basic Cookbook for Young Vegetarians by Maura D. Shaw and Sydna Altschuler. Wappingers Falls, NY: Shawangunk Press, 1994. Information on healthy eating, meal planning, and cooking techniques, as well as easy fun recipes.

Moosewood Cookbook by Mollie Katzen. Berkeley, California: Ten Speed Press, 1999. Classic creative vegetarian cookery.

New Vegetarian Cookbook by Heather Thomas. Toronto: Harper Collins Canada, 1999. Appealing veggie fare.

Simply Vegan by Debra Wasserman and Reed Mangels. Baltimore, Maryland: Vegetarian Resource Group, 1999. The "Bible" of veganism. Quick vegan meals, vegan nutrition, and cruelty-free shopping.

The Teen's Vegetarian Cookbook by Judy Krizmanic. New York: Puffin Books, 1999. Written for teens. Easy fun recipes from breakfast beverages to desserts.

Vegetarian Cooking Around the World edited by Mary Wingett. Minneapolis: Lerner Publishing Co., 1992. For kids. Recipes and information on how to plan balanced meals.

Vegetarian Cooking for Everyone by Deborah Madison. New York: Broadway Books, 1997. "The Joy of Cooking" for vegetarians.

Glossary

Agar-agar: A thickening agent made from seaweed. Used instead of gelatin in vegetarian foods.

Animal rights: The belief that animals have the right not to be exploited or killed for human use.

Blackstrap molasses: A by-product of sugar refining. A good source of iron, calcium, and other minerals.

Buckwheat: Not a grain and not related to wheat, but grain-like. Good for people who are allergic to wheat. Kasha is a cracked pre-cooked form of buckwheat.

Calcium: A mineral needed to build strong bones and teeth.

Carbohydrates: Nutrients that provide the body with energy.

Egg replacer: A substitute for eggs in cooking and baking. Commercial varieties are usually in powdered form.

Fat: A nutrient that the body needs to store energy and to help in the formation and function of healthy cells. Unhealthy when eaten in excess.

Fiber: A type of complex carbohydrate found in plant foods, needed for healthy digestion and other functions.

Fruitarian: A person who eats only fruits, nuts, and seeds.

Gelatin: A thickening agent made from animal bones. Kosher gelatin is usually vegetarian.

Genetic engineering: The practice of inserting genetic material from one organism into the genes of another organism.

Grain: The seed or fruit of a cereal plant. Includes amaranth, bulgur, corn, couscous, kamut, millet, oats, quinoa, rice, rye, spelt, teff, triticale, and wheat.

Herbivore: An organism that eats plants.

Iron: A mineral needed for healthy blood.

Lacto-ovo vegetarian: A person who eats eggs (ovo) and dairy products (lacto) but no meat, poultry, or fish.

Legume: Plants whose seeds grow in pods. Includes beans, lentils, split peas, and peanuts.

Macrobiotic diet: A diet, usually vegetarian, that follows a Japanese philosophy based on principles of eating.

Miso: A salty paste made from fermented soybeans, used to flavor soups, stews, spreads, and other dishes.

Nutritional yeast: A dietary supplement that is rich in B vitamins and has a nutty or cheese-like flavor. Not the type of yeast used to bake bread. Red Star Vegetarian Support Formula is a good source of vitamin B_{12}.

Organic: Food that has been grown or raised without the use of chemical fertilizers, herbicides, or pesticides.

Protein: A nutrient needed for growth and repair of body tissues.

Pulse: The seeds of legumes.

Rennet: A substance taken from the lining of calves' stomachs, used to thicken milk to make cheese.

Semi-vegetarian: Not a true vegetarian; a person who eats some types of meat or who eats meat occasionally.

Soy cheese: A cheese-like food made from soy milk. Can be substituted for dairy cheese.

Soy milk: A non-dairy beverage made from soybeans. Fortified soy milk can be substituted for dairy milk in a vegetarian or vegan diet.

Tahini: A spread made from ground sesame seeds.

Tamari: Naturally brewed soy sauce.

Tempeh: A high-protein food made from cultured soybeans. Can be used in sandwiches or main dishes.

Textured vegetable protein (TVP): Dried granules, flakes, or chunks made from soy flour. Reconstitutes in boiling water.

Tofu: A versatile high-protein food made from the "milk" of soybeans. Varieties thickened with calcium salts are a good source of calcium.

Vegan: A person who does not use any animal products for food or clothing.

Vegetarian: A person who eats no meat of any kind (beef, pork, lamb, poultry, or fish) but who may eat other animal products such as eggs, dairy products, and honey.

Vitamin B_{12}: A vitamin needed for a healthy nervous system.